TECHNOLOGICAL DECISIONS AND DEMOCRACY

TECHNOLOGICAL DECISIONS AND DEMOCRACY

European Experiments in Public Participation

DOROTHY NELKIN

 SAGE PUBLICATIONS   Beverly Hills/London

For information address:

SAGE PUBLICATIONS, INC.
275 South Beverly Drive
Beverly Hills, California 90212

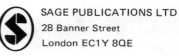

SAGE PUBLICATIONS LTD
28 Banner Street
London EC1Y 8QE

Printed in the United States of America

Library of Congress Cataloging in Publication Data

Nelkin, Dorothy.
    Technological decisions and democracy.

    Bibliography: p. 101
    1. Technology and state—Europe—Citizen participation.
I. Title.
T26.A1N44   301.24'3   77-9133
ISBN O-8039-0902-0

FIRST PRINTING

Contents

Preface

FOR SOME YEARS, I have been studying the controversies over science and technology that have developed
with increasing awareness of their social and environmental impacts. Such controversies, now even more
prominent in the dispute over recombinant DNA, have
become a major concern in the field of science and
public policy. Beyond the substantive issues underlying
the controversies lie difficult questions about the appropriate locus of authority for technical decisions with
far-reaching social consequences. In particular, they
raise questions about the role of affected citizens in the
decision-making process.

Until recently, I focused on controversies within
the United States, such as protests against construction
of nuclear power plants, airports, and other technological facilities. Public concern over such projects has led

to legislative requirements for increased public involvement in planning and decision-making. For example, the National Environmental Policy Act, the Airport and Airways Development Act, and the Water Pollution Control Act call for public hearings and other means of participation in decisions to facilitate the implementation of new technologies. This legislation also expresses an ideology—that participation is a right and a source of legitimacy in a democratic society.

Yet, implementation of participatory procedures has been a source of frustration in policy areas where technical expertise is an important resource. Difficulties are exacerbated by increasing disagreement among experts themselves over questions of risks.

This study originated with the idea that the understanding of participatory procedures might be enhanced by examining the experiences in several small European countries with more centralized and often more manageable programs. The point in studying such experiences is not to find policy models that can be uncritically transferred to the American context, but rather it is to better understand the relationship between participatory mechanisms and the political and social context in which they develop.

Research for this study involved extensive interviewing. I would like to thank the many people in Sweden, the Netherlands, and Austria who patiently cooperated in interviews and supplied crucial documents. These included people in government ministries and agencies, as well as in citizen action groups. I would especially like to thank Michael Pollak, who interviewed for me in Austria and helped with German language documents. In addition, I would like to thank Guild

Nichols, Jean-Jacques Salomon, Georges Ferné and Ari Rip for their useful criticism. I appreciate the hospitality of the Institut D'Urbanisme at Université Paris Val de Marne while doing this research. Partial support for writing up the material was provided by grants from the National Science Foundation's Science Policy Division and from the National Science Foundation-National Endowment for the Humanities EVIST program.

Introduction:

NEARLY EVERY technological development, be it the siting of a large-scale facility such as a nuclear power plant or a hospital, the implementation of a new biomedical or agricultural innovation, or a technology-based program such as fluoridation or genetic screening, is surrounded by controversy. Decisions once defined as technical are increasingly forced into the political arena by people who are skeptical about the value of technological progress, who perceive a gap between technology and human needs, or who mistrust the concentration of authority in bureaucracies responsible for technological change. Policies concerning science and technology once based on the assumption that technology equals progress now involve difficult social choices. Policy makers must establish appropriate research and development priorities while meeting conflicting demands from dif-

Participation
as an Ideology

ferent social sectors. They must define acceptable levels of risk and weigh these risks against the benefit of new technologies in the face of diverse judgments about what constitutes a "good society." And they must balance national interests with local or regional demands, practical constraints with ideological arguments, long-term concerns with short-term imperatives, technical possibilities with social considerations.

Science policy has always involved such dilemmas, but the pervasive influence of science and technology—the visibility of their social impacts—has brought growing public concern about technological development and declining confidence in the bureaucracies responsible for technical decisions. Policies once accepted with few questions as automatically in the public interest are now perceived as benefiting some at the expense of others.[1]

Contributing to skepticism is resentment of the growth of bureaucracy and the consequent "invisibility" of the power elite. The increased reliance upon technical expertise has helped to obscure responsibility for major social decisions, weakening the system of checks and balances. And policies, framed in technical language, are often difficult to comprehend or to control.[2]

Until recently, it was assumed that progress has inevitable costs and that people ought to adapt or leave (one is often reminded of Lord Coke's famous statement, made some three hundred years ago, that one ought not to have so delicate a nose that one cannot bear the smell of hogs). However, it has become difficult to avoid the burdens of technology; and, as the options decrease, the tendencies to protest increase. Indeed, those people affected by technical decisions have powerful incentives to try to influence them. Thus, people are increasingly inclined to act on their concerns about technology. "Action groups," organized to influence the implementation of particular projects, have proliferated throughout the United States and Western Europe.[3] Unwilling to accept the role of cumbersome administrative bureaucracies as representing the public interest, skeptical about technical expertise and its adequacy as a basis for policy decisions, these groups have demanded greater public access to information and broader participation in decisions concerning science and technology.[4]

Indeed, participation as an ideology seems to be of growing importance just when technical complexity threatens to limit effective political choice. The declining influence of the citizen in an expertise-based society has thus become a pervasive public concern widely interpreted as a failure in the existing system of representation. It has called for a revitalization of democratic principles and their extension to areas of sectoral and national policy where they were not formerly applied. This political challenge has stimulated a variety of experiments in "democratization"—efforts to make political systems more responsive to the general public by incorporating diverse citizen interests in the formulation and implementation of national policies for science and technology.

This book analyzes citizens' efforts to influence policies for science and technology, and government initiatives to structure ways to more directly involve the public in policy-making. The technical character of decisions in science policy, as well as their scale and high cost—requiring extraordinary public resources—poses special problems. To examine these problems, we focus on changing forms of participation in three technical policy areas: physical planning, nuclear energy policy, and research policy.

The environmental and social problems resulting from urban reconstruction gave rise in the 1960s to demands for increased local influence on physical planning. These led to administrative reforms providing for citizen input at various stages in the planning process. Later, public concerns shifted to national environmental issues, and the civilian nuclear energy program became an area of critical debate. Nuclear power appeared to many as a symbol of the Faustian implications of modern science and technology, provoking discussion of fundamental political choices that called for broad public involvement.

The allocation of research funds has become still another issue of growing public concern, as budget constraints call for a more careful structuring of priorities in the face of competing demands. Governments have thus sought ways to better inform the public about scientific and technical issues, to assess public opinion concerning science, and to broaden representation in committees dealing with research priorities.

The possible mechanisms of participation are numerous, and they vary within different national settings.[5] Formal mechanisms include public hearings and other forums that provide citizens with the opportunity to present their viewpoints before government action is taken. In the United States, these approaches are institutionalized within legislation. For example, the National Environmental Policy Act and the licensing procedures for power plant and airport construction require public hearings to assess local citizen opinion. More direct participatory mechanisms include citizen representation on the administrative boards or advisory groups of public corporations. The U.S. Congress has created an Office of Technology Assessment to provide information on the potential effects of new technologies and, thus, to allow legislators to more effectively bring their views to bear on important technological choices. Other formal channels through which citizens can express their interests include complaint or appeal systems such as the ombudsmen or the administrative courts in several European countries.

Outside the formal channels of participation are various ad hoc efforts to influence policy, reflected in the proliferation of citizen action groups in recent years. Some are temporary coalitions formed to influence or obstruct specific projects; others are more permanent interest groups with general ideological concerns (Zero

Population Growth, the Sierra Club, Friends of the Earth). They try to influence technical decisions by lobbying, litigation, petitions, technical reports, and actual physical obstruction. In the United States, the law courts have become a major channel through which aggrieved citizens or concerned organizations can bring pressure to bear on decision makers. The importance of this approach is evident in the increase in environmental litigation.[6]

A central problem, both for the ad hoc groups attempting to influence science and technology policy and the government agencies initiating participatory experiments, is how to create an informed citizenry. Mechanisms to educate the public and to communicate technical information include "public interest science," education, special television programs, data banks and exhibits, or demonstrations, among others. Such efforts can serve several objectives; they may increase direct public influence on the formation of policy, or may merely inform policy makers about public concerns. More often, they are a means to win acceptance and facilitate the implementation of decisions already made.

Experiences during the last decade have provided insights into the problems of public involvement in policy-making: the inevitable increase in disagreement as more groups become engaged in the decision-making process, the difficulty in defining legitimate representation, and the costly delays. These problems are handled in different ways in different political contexts. Governments may explore ways to open channels for public involvement as a means to seek information concerning public opinion, to manipulate the public, to contain progress, to obtain political backing in order to effect social change, or to actually distribute decision-making power.[7] Their definitions of "participation" and consequently the structure of their efforts will vary accordingly. The important question is *who is to be involved?* Professionals, administrators, industrial interests, elected representatives, or consumers? The answer will determine the values and priorities to be maximized in policy formulation.

This inquiry into public involvement in decisions relating to science and technology seeks to better understand how commitments to citizen participation are put into practice and how this is influenced by political contexts and traditional social expectations. We have selected for study the experience in three European countries: Sweden, the Netherlands, and Austria.

Policies for science and technology in these three countries have faced concerted opposition, creating a dilemma for the governing social democratic parties. The success of the Social Democrats in central and northern Europe can in part be attributed to their image as defenders of full employment and redistribution. Yet the ideology of "democratization" has also played a major role in attracting their political constituency. Once in power, the parties have sought to satisfy the expectations of both economic improvement and a more democratic, participatory society—goals that are not necessarily compatible. Questions of political authority raised in recent years by the environmental movement, and by the nuclear protest in particular, threatened the tenuous balance between these two aspects of the Social Democratic program. Moreover, public confidence in governmental capacity to respond to the environmental problems engendered by rapid growth was eroding. Occurring at a time when the parliamentary majority of the governing parties faced significant challenge, environmental issues became key factors in the political struggle for parliamentary control. Thus, when faced with criticism, the three Social Democratic governments initiated various forms of participation both as a response to political demands and as a means to stimulate social reform. Yet their different political and social traditions have led to different expectations concerning the means to incorporate diverse and often conflicting views into public policy. These differences reflect varying assumptions concerning the role of government in a democracy. Is government a means to ensure the well-being of a passive population by providing the best available leadership? Or do the principles of a democratic society require broad political participation as an end in itself?[8]

We will describe the ad hoc efforts by citizens in Sweden, the Netherlands, and Austria to influence science and technology policy, and compare the participatory techniques recently initiated by the three governments. We use the comparative context to better understand how political constraints and traditional assumptions shape the techniques of participation and the important question of who becomes involved. And this in turn may provide some insight into the problems that arise as governments and agencies try to implement their commitments to citizen participation in science and technology.

NOTES

1. See Nelkin (1975b) for discussion of the problems with respect to airports.

2. Macrae (1970).

3. For discussion of conflicts over the implementation of technological projects see Nelkin (1971, 1975a); Mazur (1975).

4. See the discussion of "Participatory Technology" in Carroll (1971). For data on public attitudes toward administrative bureaucracies in the United States, see Todd Laporte (1975).

5. See Mermin (1975) and Carroll (1971) for discussions of mechanisms used in the United States.

6. Two factors in the United States have maximized public access through the courts: first, the liberalization of the rules of "standing" to include esthetic or environmental as well as economic interests; second, the class action mechanism through which public interest centers can take legal action in the name of groups or individuals unable to bring individual law suits.

7. For a discussion of the different degrees of participation, see Arnstein (1960).

8. See extended discussion of these assumptions in Bachrach (1967). The central issue in the debates is the appropriate degree of power held by the "democratic elite"—e.g., an enlightened leadership capable of providing equality of services.

The Political

SWEDEN

SWEDEN IS A Constitutional Monarchy with a unicameral parliament; executive power rests with its cabinet. Its politics, dominated by the Social Democratic Party from 1932 to 1976, have often been characterized as a "consensus maintained by compromise" among five political parties and the major popular organizations. Over half the adult population is estimated to belong to a trade union or other associations, commonly called popular movements. These include the LO trade union (workers' federation) with about 1.5 million members, the TCO (the white-collar association) with about one-half million members, plus religious and professional organizations, and temperance groups.[1] Compromise has been achieved with relatively little conflict. The

2

Context

large and well-established popular organizations are institutionalized within the government apparatus, and represented in the Committees and Advisory Groups that guide administrative agency decisions.[2] In this corporatist state, decisions are taken by a consensus among these key interest groups; until recently, political parties played only a limited role.

There appears to be widespread trust that the public interest will be adequately reflected by the leadership of these organizations, the appointed government administrators, and the political parties. Democracy is equated more with equal and efficient distribution of public services than with political choice—a service orientation dominated more by technical rather than political values. This concept—that democracy in a welfare state is to be defined more in terms of benefits than politics, was expressed by one government spokesman as follows: "Our welfare policy has helped us to create a democracy in the true sense of the word. Everyone goes to the same public insurance benefit society."[3]

This has created a paradox. On the one hand, the concept of democratic participation in national policy-making is an essential part of the Swedish political system, institutionalized in the constitutional requirements for free access to information (Freedom of the Press Act 1949[4]), in the ombudsmen,[5] in a "remiss system in which all official proposals are circulated to interested parties within and outside the government, and in the representation of organizations in ad hoc ministerial committees.[6] On the other hand, it has often been suggested that this participatory system is used mainly by a well-established elite and that policy emerges out of a lengthy process of negotiation and compromise among relatively few leaders of the government and the major associations.

The power of this leadership has been reinforced by administrative centralization, unmitigated by any strong tradition of regional or local influence. While municipalities and regions have had independent powers of taxation and formal responsibility for self-government in specific areas since 1863, fragmentation and limited local interest in national problems has minimized local influence.[7] The political focus on national problems, a limited public interest in political decisions, and an elaborate process of assuring satisfactory compromise among powerful groups has reduced tendencies toward overt expression of political conflict..

Cabinet members and administrative agencies dominate the policy process. But in contrast to the strict

separation of powers in the United States, Swedish
government agencies responsible for executive action are
managed by boards that in some cases include political
representatives from the parliament (including members
from minority parties) and from major interest groups.
Moreover, the ministries have small staffs and rely ex-
tensively on committees that include members of unions
and political parties, as well as outside experts.[8] Opportunities for public discussion of policy options are available through the publication of minutes by the agency
boards and through the "remiss" system (which makes
automatic consultation of outside interests before parliamentary discussion). In addition, except for certain
documents which are restricted because of their relation
to national defense, all government documents are available for public scrutiny, a privilege used mainly by
journalists.[9]

An individual may appeal alleged administrative
inequities through the ombudsman. While there are
administrative courts through which individuals may
also submit complaints, a citizens group has no legal
"standing" to engage in environmental litigation.

Briefly, then, the traditional means of formal participation in the development of national policies in
Sweden proceeds as follows: A proposal from a committee, working under the terms of reference given by the
ministry, is circulated for comment to public agencies
and to the interested major associations. Various respon-
ses and the ministerial justification of the proposal then
go to the parliament, which sends them to the concerned
standing committee to negotiate a compromise among
diverse parties. This committee may call for hearings,
but it operates in secret until it finally submits a recom-

mendation to parliament. It is at this point that the committee's views and minority opinions are published and the parliament makes a decision.

In this context of well-institutionalized channels for participation of representatives of major organizations, the Swedish government has responded to challenges by seeking to extend citizen involvement in policy areas normally defined as the domain of technical expertise. For example, the mission of a new government technology assessment institution, the Secretariat of Future Studies, is to investigate ways "to broaden and deepen democracy in Swedish society."[10]

THE NETHERLANDS

Like Sweden, the Netherlands is also a Constitutional Monarchy with executive power in the cabinet. However, the Dutch parliament is bicameral. Its first chamber is elected by provincial representative councils, and its second, on the basis of proportional representation. The Dutch have also traditionally placed a high value on harmony and consensus, but from a far more fragmented and diversified base than in Sweden.[11] The Netherlands' cleavages are rooted in the original seven United Provinces, leaving a tradition of mistrust of centralized authority and, unlike Sweden, a concern for municipal autonomy. Each of the present eleven provinces has its own representative council responsible for administration and physical planning. The more than 860 municipalities have had, until recently, a great deal of local autonomy in day-to-day physical and social planning.[12]

Cleavages are accentuated by the religious divisions in the Netherlands. Two powerful religious groups predominate, the Dutch Reformed Church (38 percent of the population) and the Roman Catholic (39 percent). The division is institutionally reflected in the existence of separate newspapers, television and radio stations, schools, hospitals, and voluntary associations. People are accustomed to having their views expressed by newspapers or associations representing their special interests.

The political scene is dominated by vertical groups, the so-called "pillars." These groups, defined by a convergence of religious and political ideology, are the "supports" of the national structure and channel communications from the grass roots to the elites, who tend to negotiate among themselves to resolve conflicts and develop policies.[13] Political parties often tend to reflect more these social substructures than voter preferences. Moreover, diverse subcultures have access to the decision-making process through the electoral system by proportional representation rather than by majority rule. This guarantees easy entry of new political parties into parliament. These new parties may coalesce over particular issues or immediate goals; there are now thirteen parties in all.[14]

The interests of heterogeneous groups in Dutch society are also incorporated in the numerous advisory bodies formed to assist government ministries. Thus, the traditional style in Holland is one of accommodation to plural interests, and this has created an expectation for active citizen involvement. Critics tend to engage in direct political activity in order to influence legislation or government policies rather than to manipulate around them. And to maintain political stability, the government has sought to incorporate critical groups within the system, a practice which has helped to reduce the divisiveness of adversary politics.

It was in this pluralist context, however, that a rash of ill feeling against the establishment, particularly among young people and workers, erupted in the late 1960s. The action groups expressing these attitudes argued that the system of institutionalized accommodation of plural interests had calcified; that certain groups lacked representation; and that new problems of a rapidly changing society were neglected. A "technocratic tyranny," they claimed, was undermining local autonomy. Quite diverse action groups seeking environmental protection, industrial democracy, or university reform shared a common theme—the declining influence of the citizen.

This sentiment assumed increased importance in the early 1970s. During the parliamentary elections in April 1971, a national survey reported that 50 percent of the population claimed to have little influence on municipal politics; 59 percent agreed that political parties were interested only in votes, not in citizens' opinions; 69 percent thought they ought to have considerable influence in important public decisions; and only 9 percent felt they already had such influence.[15] This helped to shape the political mandate of the new 1973 Social Democratic government in the Netherlands—"to spread income, knowledge and power."

AUSTRIA

Austria is a federal republic based on a complex institutional scheme combining a parliamentary government with several corporate elements that form the basis of political representation. Its parliament is bicameral: The "national council" is elected on the basis of proportional representation; the "federal council" is composed of delegates elected by the nine Länder parliaments, but not necessarily drawn from members of these parliaments. The territorial division of power through the nine Länder provides opportunities for regional participation in national politics and autonomy in certain areas.[16] More important, the professional "chambers" (official associations created by public law to represent occupational interests) play a central role as channels for participation. Every person in a profession (industrial workers, peasants, industrialists, etc.) is automatically a member of a chamber, and these organizations, the private interest groups, and the trade unions not only protect the professional interests of their members, but also participate in the general political process.

The public status of the chambers guarantees that most social conflicts can be dealt with in an official framework through the so-called "Sozialpartnerschaft." The chambers have official representatives in administrative councils, and their experts participate in the discussions of parliamentary commissions. This influence is reinforced by personal relations and the fact that chamber officials often serve as government officials as well. The relationship between the parties and the chambers is very close. In fact, suborganizations of the political parties present their candidates to the chamber elections. The high majority of populists in the economic (commerce, industry) and agricultural chambers, and of socialists in the workers' chamber, reduces internal debate. This organizational network explains the high degree of social integration in Austria: Most working Austrians belong to two or three professional organizations (chambers and interest groups). The trade union has 1.5 million members; the peasant association, 400,000 members.[17]

The chamber officials are elected on the basis of the federal divisions and of proportional representation. They make official statements on behalf of their constituencies, and they must be consulted in legislative matters that bear on their interests. For example, as in Sweden, all proposed legislation passes through a "remiss" system.[18]

Any group or individual may introduce legislative proposals for parliamentary consideration by collecting 30,000 signatures requesting a national referendum. If the proposal is approved by 200,000 votes, parliament is obliged to debate the legislation. While the referendum provides possibilities for political initiative outside the organizations, it is only used to indicate the public support of specific legislation; it does not reveal opposition, nor is it binding on parliament. This referendum procedure (Volksbegehren) was first used in the early 1960s by some independent newspapers to propose a reform of the state broadcasting system. Later, in 1968, a forty-hour week referendum was initiated by the trade unions. A third referendum, against abortion, was introduced in 1974 by an association linked to the Catholic Church, in response to free abortion legislation. All of these campaigns succeeded in collecting nearly 900,000 signatures. Parliament approved the first two proposals, but rejected the third despite similar evidence of support.

Besides the extensive organization of the working

population through the associations, political party membership is also very very high. Of the 5 million voters, more than 700,000 belong to the Socialist Party and nearly one million to the Austrian People's Party.[19] Yet, these numbers do not necessarily imply a high degree of political consciousness or commitment. Rather, they reflect the considerable party influence on the professional chambers and on the state sector of the economy; party membership may influence one's professional career or provide numerous social advantages. Affiliation to one of the two parties serves as a major criterion for job distribution within the public sector, as well as for housing.[20]

In fact, the complex system of representation has created a certain depoliticization, reducing the tendency to express dissent. For, as in Sweden, policy is the result of a long process of negotiation and compromise among the elite representing participating political organizations and institutions. Also, as in Sweden, the high degree of organization and the similar mechanisms for the involvement of a representative elite in legislative matters is directed to compromise and consensus. The consensus orientation of Austrian politics is strongly reinforced by the historical experience of the civil war in 1934, "Catholic fascism" from 1934 to 1938, and National Socialism from 1938 to 1945. These authoritarian experiences, the later occupation, and the continuing threats of division created strong feelings that compromise and consensus were the only reasonable way to govern a small country. This was reflected in the coalition between the People's Party and the Socialist Party from 1945 to 1966. (The Austrian People's Party [Christian Democrats] governed Austria from 1966 to

1970, and the Socialist Party has governed since 1970.) From 1966 to 1970, the People's Party had an absolute majority in the "national council." After the spring elections of 1970, the Socialist Party formed a minority government, and has had an absolute majority since 1971. The distribution of the seats has been as follows:

TABLE 1.

	SPO (Socialist)	OVP (People's Party)	FPO (Liberal)
1966-1970	74	85	6
1970-1971	81	78	6
1971-1975	93	80	10[a]
1975	93	80	10

[a.] In 1970, an electoral reform providing almost exact proportional representation also increased the seats from 165 to 183.

Austria's system of highly institutionalized negotiation guarantees official representation. However, those who are represented sometimes have difficulty in identifying themselves with such an indirect means of participation. This was expressed in the student movement in the late 1960s and in the socialist election theme of 1970: "Democratization of all sectors of society."

NOTES

1. Elvander (1974).
2. Schiff (1975).

3. Michaneck (1963).

4. Anderson (1973).

5. Gellhorn (1966).

6. Participatory schemes are well advanced in industry. Industrial democracy has been an objective of the Social Democratic Party for years. In 1920, a party spokesman wrote: "In the long run it is impossible to preach equality in the governing of the nation—that is political democracy —and at the same time declare as unalterable an institution that within industry allows a group of owners with hereditary power to command the daily lives of thousands of workers." Quoted in Myrdal (1971).

7. Anton (1975).

8. Lundquist (1972); Caulcott and Mountfield (1974); Anton (1975). Anton describes a "hostage principle," in which association and party leaders are hostages in committees and boards, leaving little opportunity for disagreement after decisions are made by these groups. Their involvement also helps to create a sense of shared responsibility. .

9. Anderson (1973).

10. Secretariat for Future Studies (1975).

11. Den Bak (1972), Daalder and Irwin (1974).

12. Hammett (1975).

13. Thomasen (1975); Daalder and Irwin (1974); Lijphart (1968).

14. Van Putten (1974).

15. Den Bak (1972: 155).

16. The Austrian constitution defines the federal and "Länder" (state) authority in different areas. The federation has the authority for legislation and execution in areas of defense, monetary and credit policy, foreign policy, and the federal budget; there are cases in which legislation is made by the federation, but executed by the Länder (citizenship, social housing, aspects of education). In some areas, the federal government can legislate overall policy and the Länder have authority within this framework (agricultural workers, land reform). All areas not explicitly mentioned as federal authority in the constitution are under the authority of the Länder. This can create difficulties for projects that concern more than one Land, but are not defined as federal affairs. See Machek (1961: 28-30); Kostelka and Unkart (1974).

17. Ucakar (1974); Matzner (1974); Neuhauser (1966); Nuszbaumer (1973: 48).

18. This "remiss" system is only one of the possible ways to influence government. Since 1957 the "Paritätische Kommission für Preis- und Lohnfragen," composed of the chancellor, the Ministers of Interior, of Commerce and of Social Affairs, and two representatives each from the economic chamber, the agricultural chamber, the workers' chamber and the trade unions, functions as an economic authority. Its objective is voluntary control of prices and wages. In specific jurisdictions—i.e., in the

labor courts and the commercial courts—the chambers are represented by their experts. See Ucakar (1974: 417-419)

19. See Oberleitner (1972).

20. The importance of the parties for everyday life is also enhanced by their organizational structure: the Socialist Party has eighteen suborganizations (for youth, retirees, home-renters, sportsmen, singers, fishermen, intellectuals, etc.), the Populist Party has eleven suborganizations covering the same population groups. Oberleitner (1972); Lehmbruch (1967).

Political Demands

SWEDEN

IN THE EARLY 1970s, action groups in Sweden began to question the effectiveness of the well-organized system of public representation. The large popular organizations were indeed well represented in government decisions, but they themselves were said to lack internal democracy and to foster a passive membership.[1] Moreover, a tradition of cooperation between private industry and government limited actual consultation, especially in technological matters, to a specialized elite.[2] Little consideration was given to developing an informed citizenry. For example, when the 1972 Royal Commission on Environmental Research stressed the need to disseminate research results, it defined the consumers of research as government authorities and indus-

for Participation

try, but made no mention of the public.[3] Yet, because of the many institutional safeguards for democracy, technological decisions appeared to be the result of a broad consensus.[4]

The growing popularity of the Center Party (formerly the Farmers' Party) implied increasing public concern with questions of participation, especially with respect to bureaucratic and technical decisions. Between 1968 and 1973, this party, advocating decentralized decision-making with greater public involvement, greatly increased its popular support. The Social Democratic Party won 50.1 percent of the popular vote in 1968; 43.6 percent in 1973. The Center Party won 15.7 percent in 1968 and 25.1 percent in 1973. By the election of 1976, the 350 parliamentary seats were split as follows:

Social Democrats	44.6 percent
Center Party	25.7 percent
Conservatives	14.6 percent
Liberals	9.7 percent
Communists	5.4 percent

The Center Party leader became Prime Minister, interrupting 44 years of Social Democratic leadership.

The growth of the Center Party reflects in part the very rapid social mobility in Sweden. Many white-collar workers, for example, are children of farmers. Despite their occupational shift, they continue to vote with the Center Party (old Farmers' Party) as a part of their tradition. This reinforces the appeal of its anti-bureaucracy position.

The popularity of the Center Party also reflected a sense of political alienation in the municipalities. In 1952, there were some 2,500 municipalities, each with elected representatives on local committees and various governing bodies. Over the next twenty years, a series of mergers reduced the number of municipalities to 278. The purpose of the mergers was to create municipal units large enough to have a sizeable budget and a civil service with technical competence to provide local services.[5] Aimed at improving the efficiency of local government performance, the mergers also increased the power of the administrative bureaucracy. In the process, they inevitably reduced the influence of many elected officials and the personal contact between citizens and local government. While there is no strong tradition of aggressive local community organization in Sweden, the growing distance between citizens and government that followed the mergers contributed to the growing anti-bureaucracy ideology. Concern with these changes in the political structure coincided with demands from the environmental movement.

THE GREEN WAVE

Environmental protection is a deep-rooted value among the Swedish people, who have long been concerned with leaving nature undisturbed.[6] Thus, as an environmental movement developed, it had strong local backing. Public awareness of health-related aspects of environmental problems in Sweden was aroused in the mid-1960s with respect to mercury pollution, a serious problem given the size of the pulp and paper industry.[7] Other issues, such as DDT, came on the policy agenda as the press tuned into international environmental concerns and environmental action groups began to form.

Urban redevelopment in Stockholm during the late 1960s provided the first target for the so-called "green wave," as activists formed neighborhood groups to oppose specific projects (e.g., a housing development called Skärholmen). The green wave peaked during the "battle of the elms" in 1971—a series of demonstrations over a plan to excavate a popular tree-lined square in central Stockholm for a subway. This plan had moved through the usual elaborate decision-making process and had been approved by many agencies and organizations. Once it had been approved, six months of demonstrations, petitions, and rallies failed to influence the plans. Artists painted the trees, poets wrote poems about them, architects devised alternate plans for the subway, and the media picked up the issue, supporting the opposition. The decision remained firm. Then, during one week, a group of students "occupied" the elms, physically guarding them, as thousands of people gathered in the square. The mood of a popular festival was, however, darkened by violence. At the end of this week, officials agreed to reconsider the issue and eventually the subway plan was changed.[8]

The issue of the elms itself was marginal, but it catalyzed a major discussion about the quality of life in Sweden and about the role of local citizens in influencing plans affecting their neighborhoods. The government had based its agenda on technical questions relating to its provision of services; how to accommodate increased traffic with minimum cost; how to meet the service needs of commuters. The action groups raised political questions. Was an increase in traffic desirable? What would be the social costs? Could alternatives adequately meet social needs? And, above all, who should make the decision?

Since the "battle of the elms" and the subsequent proliferation of action groups aimed at contesting government policies, often in ways contrary to normal political expectations, planners and politicians have been more sensitive to the possibility of protest. They ask themselves, "Will it become another battle of the elms?"

As the environmental movement in Sweden developed, conventional institutional channels began to adapt to the new concerns. Environmental legislation of 1969 set up two alternative ways in which a developer can get his project approved by the government. He may go to the Franchise Board, which, after long deliberation, will lay out the conditions of construction based on the best available means to minimize pollution. Once established, the permit is granted for ten years. Alternatively, he may go to the Environmental Protection Board, which can give the developer dispensation—i.e., free him from the necessity of getting a permit. This is a quick process, but the conditions to avoid pollution are laid out only for several months, and the developer may be called back at any time and required to update his technology if innovation makes the conditions obsolete.

Activists soon began to criticize these channels as inadequate as a means to reflect public concerns. For example, Björn Gillberg, a popular environmentalist once called the "Swedish Ralph Nader," attempted to change industrial practices concerning food additives through conventional complaint channels (the ombudsman). Failing to obtain an adequate response, he decided that "the only way to make a politician do something is to make him feel that he will lose the next election." So he devoted his time to influencing public opinion on environmental questions, writing newspaper articles and popular books, and organizing the Environmental Center in Uppsala to provide "the ordinary citizen with information on environmental problems in plain Swedish."[9]

For a brief period, his efforts were remarkably popular. A poll in 1974 by the Swedish Institute for Opinion Research (SIFO) indicated that people had more faith that Gillberg would look after their interests than they had in either the consumer ombudsman or the Office of Consumer Affairs.[10]

Environmentalists have tried to adopt the American practice of protest by employing legal action against the government concerning the siting of a power plant at Ringhals. (The use of the courts is not a customary means of protest in the Swedish system.) Furthermore, they have made political demands to extend direct citizen involvement in a government that, they claim, "would like to run the country without too much interference from ordinary citizens." The ombudsman, according to some critics, serves mainly "to legalize the policy of the establishment." The Freedom of the Press Act is useful, but "passive."

The difficulty in taking legal action is a further barrier; it is not possible to go to an administrative court unless one is directly affected by an administrative decision. Moreover, in a small country, it is difficult to find experts who are not already part of the establishment. In brief, certain environmentalists argued that despite the government's commitment to participation, Sweden remains a "closed system" dominated by "collusion" between industry and government.

The environmental movement thus turned from concern with specific environmental problems to demands for changes in the structure of power through greater incorporation of public influence. Ironically, the movement split in late 1975, because of the lack of democracy within Gillberg's organization. Many of the original participants in the battle of the elms had a more radical perspective, seeking major changes in Sweden's economic and political system. Gillberg, they claim, had built a "despotic empire," preventing the participation of groups who disagreed with his strategy. Gillberg, in turn rejects his critics as "left-wing" and counterproductive in the effort to expand citizen influence.

The growing concern with political authority on the part of all factions in the movement gradually became a source of political discomfort for the government. The evolution of the Swedish environmental movement and its influence on government policy is best perceived through the nuclear debate, the most important environmental action since the "battle of the elms," and one that provoked a similar broad-ranging discussion about the future of Swedish society.

THE ANTI-NUCLEAR MOVEMENT

With its cold climate and technology-intensive industry, Sweden has high per capita energy needs. Yet it has no known natural gas or oil reserves, and its hydro-power resources have largely been exploited. Thus, it is heavily dependent upon imported oil. Sweden does, however, have uranium reserves and is anxious to develop a nuclear program.

Its nuclear research program began after World War II, on a small scale within the Swedish defense program. In 1948, it was transferred to a semi-public corporation, AB Atomenergi, with industrial and government collaboration. When the first reactor went critical in 1954, Sweden embarked on a natural uranium heavy-water reactor program, a choice intended to allow self-sufficiency using Swedish uranium deposits. The safety problems of an expanding nuclear program were not widely discussed; the only controversial questions related to the balance of private versus public control.

The first major nuclear project, the Swedish-designed Agesta nuclear power station, built in one of the suburbs of Stockholm, caused a violent debate in the early 1960s. The debate centered around the health hazards from radioactive release during normal operation. Professor Linus Pauling, of the United States, was called in as a witness in the lawsuit. The station proceeded to open, and the debate subsided. But the station was closed in 1974 for financial reasons.

The Marviken station, intended to be operative in 1968, was technically too ambitious. It could not meet the safety requirements without major alterations, which could not be financially justified.[11] When it was finally abandoned in 1970, its costs had mounted to about $100,000,000 of which only a minor part could be reclaimed. The technology developed for Marviken was to be used in the Swedish light water power reactor program. Thus, the failure of Marviken had some important political consequences. One of the more influential persons who was engaged in the discussions of Marviken was the Nobel Prize winner Hannes Alfvén, who was at the beginning one of the supporters of the project, but later became a strong opponent.

The public debate began on a local level in 1969 over the future use of a site near Gothenburg acquired by AB Atomenergi in the early 1960s as suitable for a reprocessing plant. Groups from the University of Gothenburg took a very active part in the debate, which comprised several factors, such as interference with a coastal recreation area, health hazards of reprocessing, and the danger of processing plutonium. Plans to use this site were abandoned.[12]

In 1970 and 1971, the Riksdag approved plans to develop eleven nuclear power plants by 1980 without too much debate. In 1971, a motion was presented to the parliament to open up discussions of energy planning to the political parties, but the motion was defeated. In 1972, a Center Party member of parliament raised questions about the "moral defensibility" of a nuclear program that could place difficult burdens on future generations. A moratorium on the construction of new power plants was suggested, but was rejected by parliament. In the same year, the Central Power Supply Administration, responsible for coordinating electric supply, published a study estimating that twenty-four reactors (an additional thirteen plants) totalling 24,000 megawatts would be needed by 1990. The program was referred to in the government bill to the Riksdag in the beginning of 1973, although no decisions were asked for at that time. The content of the study, however, met with considerable opposition inside as well as outside the Riksdag. Anti-nuclear books appeared, and environmental groups lobbied parliament more actively. The Environmental Center took legal action against the plans for a nuclear plant in Ringhals, and the Friends of the Earth collaborated with local citizens to obstruct preliminary plans to build a plant twenty miles south of Stockholm.

By 1973, the Social Democratic Party's major support in Parliament had changed to equilibrium (175-175) between the blocs. At this time, the strongest opposition group, the Center Party, attacked the nuclear power program as a symbol of bureaucratic centralization and an example of government paternalism. (One headline read "Revolt Against Daddy—Say No to Nuclear Power." It became apparent that a large part of the Swedish population might be opposed to the construction of additional nuclear power plants. In February 1974, when a survey suggested that half the Swedish population opposed the construction of additional nuclear power plants, policy makers concluded that efforts must be made to involve the public more directly in nuclear decisions.

THE NETHERLANDS

Similar demands for broader public involvement in government policy-making developed in the Netherlands, where high population density (360 habitants per square kilometer) has accentuated the impact of technological change. Until the mid-1960s, the urgency of postwar reconstruction and the first benefit of prosperity overshadowed the environmental or social impacts of rapid development. However, the largest cities in the Netherlands were experiencing problems of noise, heavy traffic, air pollution, and waste disposal; and the environmental movement began to assume greater political significance.

ENVIRONMENTAL POLITICS

The environmental movement in the Netherlands is a coalition made up of many different action groups that had formed to obstruct specific projects—the siting of a chemical plant near Amsterdam, the extension of a subway, the location of blast furnaces in Rotterdam, a second national airport, the building of a dam across the Oosterschelde. By 1970, these action groups clustered in two major blocks: The Foundation for Nature and the Environment, a coalition including about 100,000 members, operates as a pressure group for specific conservation projects; the Federation of Environmental Defense describes itself as reflecting the "Club of Rome" approach and seeks basic changes in the country's socioeconomic structure as a means to resolve environmental problems.[13]

Unlike Sweden, the activities of the Netherlands' environmental groups are reinforced by an active movement among scientists concerned with "social responsibility."[14] Two federations of scientists, each with about 1,000 members, publish articles aimed at informing the public on controversial technical questions. Some groups of students and scientists have set up "shops" to advise citizens on local issues. Another indication of concern is represented by 130 scientists within Philips Research Laboratories, who meet regularly to discuss the social implications of research within this corporation, which employs some 600 scientists in all.

The environmental movement has also attracted a number of "professional protesters," who frequently appear at meetings and public hearings, since, in the Netherlands, participation in action groups is seen as a means of political mobility. Members of such groups often serve in advisory councils, using this route for a potential career in politics in one of the thirteen political parties. Significantly, three people from the environmental movement, or from parties concerned with environmental issues, have become cabinet ministers in the present government.

The Dutch environmentalists, however, face an ambivalent public. Popular books like Rachel Carson's *Silent Spring* and the Club of Rome's *Limits to Growth* have a higher per capita sales in the Netherlands than in any other country, suggesting broad public interest in environmental issues. Yet, as in most countries, there remains considerable anxiety about employment and prosperity, as well as environmental preservation. A popular slogan of one action group—"No Prosperity Without Well-Being"—is countered by another—"No Well-Being Without Prosperity"—as "democratic well-being preachers" confront the "technocratic prosperity promoters."

This ambivalence became clear when the Foundation for Nature and the Environment, concerned with eutrophication and pollution, organized a protest against the construction of a dike to close off the Oosterschelde. The people living in the area supported the construction to prevent flooding. Their safety concerns dominated their environmental interests, resulting in a long dispute. Several technical alternatives (a half-open dam, or a system to raise existing dikes) have been explored as a result of the public discussion.

By 1973, the nuclear energy program became a central target of the environmental groups. As in Sweden, the issue symbolized many general concerns; the social problems arising from rapid technological change, the inaccessibility of bureaucracies, the potential damage to the environment, and fear of nuclear proliferation.

THE NETHERLANDS' NUCLEAR DEBATE

Developing nuclear power is of somewhat less immediate urgency in the Netherlands than in Sweden since the discovery of natural gas reserves, allowing the substitution of this fuel for coal and oil and providing an estimated 25-year reserve for household needs. The Netherlands began its nuclear program through collaboration with the Norwegians in 1951. By the end of 1973, two nuclear power plants were in operation, a small 55-megawatt boiling water reactor located in Dodewaard, and a pressure water reactor of 477 megawatts in Borssele. In 1974, a White Paper from the Ministry of Economic Affairs announced the intention to build three more plants of 1,000 megawatts each by 1985. The Netherlands also had joined the Kalkar Project in 1967 (the joint liquid metal fast breeder reactor project with Germany, Belgium, and Luxembourg), and in 1971, the ultra-centrifuge project for uranium enrichment (with Germany and the United Kingdom).

Interest in the nuclear issue remained primarily within the scientific community until 1973, when parliament voted for a surtax of 3 percent on all electricity bills, specifically in order to support the Netherlands' share in the development of the multinational Kalkar Reactor Project. The surtax, implemented at a time of considerable newspaper discussion about the controversial dimensions of the nuclear program, created sudden public awareness of the issue. Thousands of citizens refused to pay the surtax. The government permitted those who objected to pay a 15 guilder fee in order to divert the 3 percent surcharge to a general energy fund, not to be used for nuclear purposes. About 5,000 people chose this option, but 1,900 continued to refuse to pay any surcharge at all. The important point, however, is that the "stop Kalkar movement" gained considerable visibility, and the nuclear program, in turn, became a major political issue.

The Minister of Economic Affairs, responsible for

the nuclear program, formed an advisory group at the beginning of 1974, including several industrial leaders, a former head of the trade unions, and a former chairman of the European Community to assist him in writing the White Paper dealing with the energy situation in the Netherlands. Several members of this advisory group, opposed to nuclear power, leaked a draft of this analysis to the anti-nuclear work lobby. The White Paper favored the nuclear program, claiming that with careful development there would be few risks. The public, it was argued, must learn to live with nuclear power.

In the summer of 1974, the original nuclear work team had organized a "reflection group" of 23 concerned people to examine and develop their preliminary report. This group included a science writer, several scientists, including members of TNO (the largely government-supported organization for applied scientific research), two parliamentarians, and several industrialists from Philips and Unilever (among the largest of the multinational corporations in the Netherlands). Their final report appeared in September of 1974 (strategically planned for release one week before the publication of the White Paper on nuclear policy by the Ministry of Economic Affairs). The reflection group's report presented social and economic aspects of the decision, evaluating the cost and benefits of four alternative policies; to expand the nuclear program, to abandon it completely, to proceed on an experimental basis with several plants, or to allow for a five-year reflection period "for a serious re-thinking of the basis of national growth and energy planning."[15] It recommended the last course, calling attention to disagreements among experts on both technical and economic dimensions of the program, and to conservation measures that could eventually influence energy needs.

After this "Reflection Paper" appeared, the press published a petition for a moratorium signed by 1,200 scientists and other public figures, including the President of the Academy of Sciences and several parliamentarians. In addition, 33 scientists and theologians from both the Protestant and Catholic Church and from diverse political persuasions publicly supported a second paper by the reflection group. This latter paper was published just before the Council of Ministers had to make a final decision on the nuclear power plants.

The Council of Ministers decided to postpone a decision pending three additional studies on health, safety, and siting problems. These studies appeared in 1975 with positive, though somewhat qualified support of the nuclear program. Meanwhile, the reflection group devoted itself to political activities, presenting complaints to the administrative court mostly on technicalities of nuclear planning. One complaint, for example, criticized the administration for putting a reactor safety report in German instead of in Dutch, and thereby making it inaccessible to the public. These complaints were all rejected by the court, though they had some influence (safety reports are now in Dutch). The reflection group also examined assumptions concerning cost and employment aspects of alternative energy sources (comparing nuclear power, oil, and coal) in order to present options for public discussion.

In January 1976, the Council of Ministers finally decided to postpone presenting the issue to parliament until after the next national elections. Although about 30 percent of the decisions taken in the Council of

Ministers are approved by parliament, this issue was less than certain, for the anti-nuclear groups included broad representation from the scientific, political, and religious communities. Moreover, people at the projected sites of the new plants were increasingly negative.

For purposes of this book, the nuclear debate in the Netherlands had several interesting dimensions. The anti-nuclear groups included many people from within the establishment, and in fact nuclear issues were often fought out within the cabinet. Respected members of the scientific community signed petitions and anti-nuclear appeals, which gave political legitimacy to the movement. The major newspapers in the Netherlands also assumed an active position critical of nuclear power and giving front-page coverage to reports of problems, but little or no attention to arguments in support of the nuclear program. The prevailing attitude of the media was evident in an incident in 1976, when the badges of two guards at a nuclear plant indicated that they had received a heavy dose of radiation. The press played up the incident to indicate the problems of nuclear power. Several days later, it was discovered that the whole event had been a practical joke; the guards had laid their badges deliberately on a radiation source to see what would happen. This discovery was only briefly reported, in the back pages of the newspapers. Such pressures combined to convince the government to take steps to open the decision-making process to greater public involvement.

AUSTRIA

Austria's Socialist Party won the elections in 1970 in part because of its promises concerning increased democratization. The division of power and the distribution of jobs and influence during the period of the coalition between Socialists and the People's Party had created a feeling, especially among the younger generation, of political impotence. Compromise was not regarded as a virtue by the generation which had not experienced the divisive strains of the postwar occupation. The demands for increased public participation in Austria, as in the Netherlands, were first reflected in the student movement and in concerns about neighborhood control over the local environment.

LOCAL CONTROL

Participatory demands began to crystallize around local planning issues in the early 1970s, when various urban renewal and transportation projects provoked public efforts to influence planning decisions. Public discussions and initiatives succeeded in influencing plans for urban highways in Graz and Bregenz in the beginning of the 1970s. In 1973, the city of Vienna organized a referendum to assess whether a research center should be built in a small park. (The park, in an affluent area of Vienna, was eventually preserved.)

A public action against urban renewal took place in Spittelberg, a small working-class enclave within a generally affluent section of Vienna. In 1974, some architects, concerned primarily with the esthetic importance of the neighborhood, created an association to obstruct plans to reconstruct the area. Then, in May 1975, an action group in Spittelberg tried to organize the people in the neighborhood to defend their own local interests. They held a four-day fair, with films and discussions with local politicians concerning the problems of urban renewal. After the fair, a group of people spontaneously occupied the empty house (owned by the city) in which the fair had been held, demanding that the city give it to the community for a political center. City officials complied and later abandoned the original urban renewal project. In fact, the city of Vienna declared this community center one of its cultural projects and agreed to restore the house according to the wishes of the action group, an example of the general tendency to incorporate radical protest into official policy. Like Stockholm's "battle of the elms," this incident generated a great deal of publicity and became a symbol of the desirability of increased local autonomy.

The economic importance of tourism has reinforced the demands of such local groups, strengthening legal measures both for the protection of neighborhoods and for the environment. Some of the largest private associations in Austria are explicitly concerned with conservation of nature. The largest of these is Naturfreunde, with more than 80,000 members. Yet most of the citizen groups' activities were less intense in Austria than in other countries, relying heavily instead on the existing channels of participation through the chambers, the associations, and the political parties. Even "radical" or "protest" groups tended to "walk on two legs," protesting outside the institutions through newspapers or petitions, while trying at the same time to influence the large, established, interest organizations. The major example of their efforts to influence government policy occurred as a result of the plans for nuclear power.

THE NUCLEAR DEBATE

In Austria, public electric companies within each Land are responsible for the energy supply, while the national company (verbundgesellschaft) is responsible for the transportation and interstate exchange of energy. The decision to use nuclear energy in the mid-1960s led to the establishment of a special nuclear energy enterprise (Kern Kraftwerksplanungsgesellschaft). This company chose the location of the first power plant in 1968 in Zwentendorf and met essentially no local resistance. The only resistance at this stage came from the medical profession in the form of an anti-nuclear memorandum, signed by 37 physicians and medical researchers and 26 other scientists, mostly biologists.[16] The limited response reflected both the relatively low sensitivity of the population to the nuclear issue at this time, as well as the economic situation of the specific community. In 1968, the issue of nuclear power was defined as a technological problem. When asked to consider the decision, the mayor of Zwentendorf, claimed to be technically incompetent and passed responsibility on to the construction council of the government of the Land an unusual abandonment of political autonomy suggesting the problematic relationship between administrative power and technical competence. The acceptance of the plant was also influenced by local economic factors. Zwentendorf, in the Northeast of Vienna, is a village which had lost its industrial importance after the war. The power plant fostered the hope of an industrial renewal and an increase in the local budget.

Quite a different situation prevailed when the government decided, in 1973, to locate a second power plant in Sankt Panthaleon at the edge of a highly industrialized area. Sankt Panthaleon is located in Linz-Enns-Wels, in the valley of the Danube, with a population of more than 300,000 people. Steel and chemical industries are predominant, and water and air pollution are major problems. By 1973, the increasing discussion about the safety and pollution problems of nuclear power provoked a strong public initiative against the proposed power plant. Protest was reinforced by the success of another battle over a hydroelectric plant in the valley of the Enns. The public initiative against this hydroelectric plant occurred just before the elections for the parliament of the Land (Upper Austria) in 1973, and politicians of all parties used it as an election issue. This widely publicized affair suggested that public initiatives could win against economic and administrative power. Thus, independent organizations concerned with preservation of nature (for example, Naturfreunde) were ready to join the movement against the power plant at Sankt Panthaleon. A nature conservation meeting in Wels in 1974 passed a resolution against nuclear energy. And, as in Sweden, the anti-nuclear movement gained the support of an influential Nobel Prize winner, Konrad Lorenz.

Yet many people living in Sankt Panthaleon remained ambivalent. The mayor, for example, expressed local sentiments when he said, "If a power plant has to be built in this region, I want it to happen in my municipality. If we have to bear the risks, we want at least to have the advantages [i.e., increased tax income]."[17] In fact, the resistance against the power plant was stronger in the neighboring communities than in Sankt Panthaleon itself.

During the protest in Sankt Panthaleon (well-publicized on television), a similar action took place on Austria's western border against plans to locate a nuclear power plant in Switzerland, only a few kilometers away from Austria. Politicians from all parties supported the action groups fighting this plan. This dispute also provoked discussion on television and in the major newspapers, and won the interest of the environmental associations. If, in a small country like Austria, a local affair is taken up by television or newspapers with a nationwide distribution, the affair automatically tends to become a "national" issue. Thus, the anti-nuclear movement gained a growing constituency.

In early 1975, a newspaper[18] organized a public discussion involving the participation of the Federal Chancellor Bruno Kreisky, and the Minister of Industry, Josef Staribacher. This first confrontation between local anti-nuclear groups and political officials was televised, giving the anti-nuclear campaign even more nationwide publicity. Its organizers collected 60,000 signatures against the power plant in the region of Sankt Panthaleon.

Austria's administrative licensing procedure allows individuals adjacent to a proposed site to appeal. The anti-nuclear forces, however, used more public channels of protest; the national media, public discussions, petitions, and confrontation with government officials. These adversary tactics, unusual in the Austrian political climate, influenced the official policy of the government. In the summer of 1975, the Chancellor announced that such a controversial and important issue

needed public discussion and could not be treated only
by the experts.

NOTES

1. Elvander (1974); Castles (1975).

2. Ninety-five percent of industry in Sweden remains in private hands.

3. Lundquist (1974b).

4. Hancock (1972).

5. There are 23 County Councils with responsibility mainly for medical services. Municipal councils are responsible for education and social services. Both units have the right to levy taxes. (Ericson, 1976).

6. Environmental problems seem less urgent in Sweden than in other countries, for it has a population of only about 8 million people in an area the size of France. This is an average of 20 people per square kilometer. In the South, however, there are 40 people per square kilometer.

7. Lundquist (1972).

8. Passow (1973); Anton (1975).

9. Gillberg (1974).

10. The poll, in March 1974, was as follows:

	Dept. of Consumer Affairs	Ombudsman	Gillbert
Strong trust	44 percent	51 percent	59 percent
Little trust	16 percent	14 percent	12 percent

SIFO suggested that Gillberg's greater aggressiveness and personal engagement in the environmental and consumer movement had helped to inspire confidence among those who knew about him. The statistics also were interpreted to reflect the loss of confidence in bureaucratic institutions.

11. Garris (1975).

12. Svedin (1975).

13. Hexstra (1973).

14. Rip and Boeker (1975).

15. Reflection Group (1975).

16. Arzte (1970). The scientific debate in Austria pitted physicists (generally supportive of nuclear energy) against biologists and medical

researchers (mostly opposed to the program). The scientific personnel of an important biological research institute ("Ludwig Boltzmann Institute für Umweltwissenschaften un Naturschutz") has actively supported the action groups, and arguments concerning the long-term genetic effects of radiation play an important role in the Austrian discussion. See: Weish and Gruber (1974, 1975).

17. The mayor made this statement in a television interview during a communal election campaign. The elections did not change the composition of the community council.

18. This newspaper, *Oberösterreichische Nachricten,* is the most important one in the Land where Sankt Panthaleon is located. It is also distributed outside the Land and is perceived as one of the influential independent newspapers in Austria.

Participatory

BY EXPERIMENTS in participation, we refer to conscious efforts by national governments to promote broader public involvement in policy-making.[1] A number of such efforts are under way throughout the United States and Western Europe. While they represent a response to demands from activist groups, these demands often reach receptive political leaders, who see increased public involvement as a means to implement their own policies for social and technological change in the face of powerful vested interests.

There are many degrees of public involvement. At one extreme are expanded public relations programs. (Electricité de France distributes comic strips on the benefits of nuclear power to elementary school children and elegant brochures on the development of new towns at power plant sites to adults.) In other cases, gov-

Experiments

ernments have provoked discussion of the political and economic problems involved in specific technological choices. Germany, for example, is trying to create a "citizens' nuclear energy dialogue" with the intention of "raising the debate onto a political level" and thereby to restore declining public confidence. "The aim of this Government campaign is to strengthen the confidence of the population in the ability of the democratic process to function especially in the controversy over nuclear energy, or to restore such confidence wherever it may be undermined."[2]

Similarly, in the United States, "science for the citizen," once a slogan of radical scientists, has been institutionalized in a National Science Foundation program designed to enable public interest groups to acquire necessary technical expertise to deal with the science and technology aspects of public policy issues.[3] In many countries, citizens are increasingly serving on boards, committees, and advisory groups of ministries and agencies responsible for science and technology policy.

Most efforts to foster participation in technical areas emphasize education. Those of interest here are directed less toward simply providing information than toward creating an informed citizenry able to engage knowledgeably in the political choices of a technological society. Most such efforts are just beginning, as governments seek ways to meet the public demands that develop out of the environmental and nuclear movements. Therefore, in our discussion of specific experiments in the Netherlands, Sweden, and Austria, we have focused on the way participatory experiments are organized, their intentions, and their assumptions about who should participate in the policy process. We will first discuss efforts to expand public involvement in technology policy, focusing on nuclear energy and the related area of physical planning, and second describe efforts to expand representation in science policy decisions.

SWEDEN

TECHNOLOGY POLICY

In the beginning of 1974, the Swedish government decided to initiate a major experiment in public education and consultation in the area of energy. The mechanism for such an experiment existed in the "study circles," a system of small study groups managed by the political parties and the major popular organizations (trade unions, temperance groups and religious groups) and financed principally with government funds.[4] The study circles date back to the end of the nineteenth century as a vehicle to develop political democracy. In the present context, the government provides factual information on subjects as requested by various organizations, and also funds for them to develop material reflecting their own concerns. Ten associations in Sweden run study circles. In order to receive support from the ministry for the groups, they must be able to provide 50,000 study circle hours per year. Thus they tend to be very large and well-established organizations. (One organization runs about 2 million study circle hours per year.) Each course must run for about twenty hours, with five to ten participants in each circle. The curriculum varies and must be approved by the director of the association. Until 1974, study circles generally focused on nontechnical issues, although some were related to current policy concerns (collective bargaining, how to participate in local political work, the reform of the working environment, and the organization of television).

In May 1974, the Riksdag approved a government proposal to sponsor study circles in the field of energy. This decision reflected an open recognition that this area, usually considered only within the ministries and mostly in terms of technical questions, should be discussed from the diverse ideological perspectives of political and social interest groups.[5] Ten organizations were invited to participate, and seven accepted; the LO (the major union) ran 3,000 circles; the ABF (run by the

Social Democrats) sponsored 4,500 circles; two Folks Schools (run by the Center and Liberal parties) sponsored 2,000 each; the Conservatives sponsored 500; and adult education groups run by the temperance movements and the Church of Sweden organized several hundred others. Each circle had between ten and fifteen members who met together for at least ten hours. About 80,000 people participated in all. The Ministries of Education and Industry gave the organizations funds to hire experts, train leaders, recruit participants and develop their own material in addition to what was provided by the government. The entire cost of this educational program came to about $650,000.

The study circles generally covered several questions—e.g., the demand for energy, the balance between different energy sources, and the implications for safety. Each was discussed in the context of political choices (e.g., the level of acceptable risk, the tradeoff between environment and consumption factors, etc.). The study material, as well as the procedures for discussion, differed greatly among the organizations.

Government officials expected that increased participation would create more favorable public attitudes toward nuclear power. In fact, one government review of a series of public hearings held after the study circles argued that the debates enhanced public sympathy for the government position. The "concrete arguments [of experts]," claimed the review, "carried most weight" for the activist groups had problems with the pragmatic arguments underlying the nuclear program.[6] Yet the reports from the study groups suggest continued uncertainty and confusion as participation broadened beyond the limited group of people who are usually interested in such issues.[7]

When the government's Energy Policy Bill was put forward, the organizations that had conducted the study circles summarized their major conclusions and released the results to the opposition political parties, who took the following positions: The Conservatives remained pro-nuclear. The Liberals agreed to continue with the existing program, in which eleven reactors would be either operating or under construction, but wanted to postpone expansion of the program until 1978. The Center Party leadership maintained its position of total opposition to any expansion beyond the five reactors already operating, and thought these, too, should eventually be closed in combination with efforts to create a low-energy society. The Communist Party also opposed the program.

A survey later suggested that attitudes within each party were more divided than the leadership opinion had indicated.[8] Public attitudes were far from definitive: 28 percent of the respondents were opposed to any nuclear power at all, and 37 percent would accept it only as a last resort. Only 21 percent felt that nuclear power was actually needed, and 14 percent did not know. An inquiry into the direct effect of the study circles on attitudes suggested only slight differences in opinion between those who participated and those who did not.

An evaluation by the National Board of Civic Information in the fall of 1974 suggested that many participants were more confused after they took part in the study circles than they had been before. Increased knowledge contributed to uncertainty and indecision; the number of persons in study circles who could decide neither for nor against nuclear power increased from 63 to 73 percent. Most could accept the existing situation, but were opposed to any change.

In March 1975, the government presented a bill which proposed a cautious nuclear policy, one that reflected public concerns about safety as well as the government's objective to maintain full employment and independence from foreign energy resources. In addition to the eleven reactors already approved, two would be added by 1985, to be located on sites which had already been approved. An active conservation program would attempt to limit the growth of energy needs to an average of 2 percent a year, with the intention of reaching zero energy growth by 1990. About $90 million were appropriated to subsidize energy research and development, out of which $40 million were directed toward conservation measures. In May 1975, 700 scientists signed a petition supporting the government proposal, and a divided parliament passed the recommendations, with intent to review the nuclear policy again in 1978. Meanwhile, of course, the elections of September 1976 displaced the Social Democratic government in an upheaval that has been attributed in large part to resistance to its nuclear program.

The government has also tried to introduce ways to increase direct local participation in physical planning.[9] In 1972, anticipating problems that might arise from the merging of municipalities, a commission on communal democracy in the Swedish Ministry of Communes recommended efforts to "revitalize democracy" in the regions and municipalities. Sweden had traditionally had procedures to involve the public in local and regional planning. Local planning authorities must consult organizations and individuals with special interests in the particular area and must exhibit regional plans for three months, and other plans for three weeks. People directly affected must have written notification, and they have a right to appeal. This procedure is limited because plans are circulated only after they are well developed. While the public is informed, there are few possibilities for actual influence.

To improve this system, the Ministry of Communes offered to pay for any experiments in participation initiated by municipal governments. There followed a series of efforts to encourage collaboration among scientists, architects, and the public through exhibits of plans and through public discussions. Some local governments set up special consultative procedures with local area councils and popular associations. But often participation in these projects was limited to villa owners and other upper-income people who were not fully representative of affected interests. Thus, recent proposals have included the creation within the communities of smaller neighborhoods, each with special councils to discuss local issues.

SCIENCE POLICY

Parallel efforts are taking place to broaden representation in decisions concerning scientific research and development. By the mid-1960s, the demands of the welfare state began to bear on science policy, reflected in the establishment of a sectoral research organization. Research and development became associated with the functions of independent administrative agencies (e.g., in defense, energy, agriculture, medicine, and housing). [10]

During the late 1960s, the problems associated with establishing R&D priorities called attention to the lack of public representation in education and research. The Swedish government is trying to democratize the university in its educational functions through the 1975 Higher Education Act (to be implemented as of July 1977). The purpose of the university reforms is to permit "a more equitable allocation of influence and opportunity" by catering education to broader public interests and by assuring that the public would have a decisive influence on the distribution of education at large. The system is being decentralized, so that in each of the six educational regions there will be a regional board which will coordinate planning and, to some extent, the distribution of resources. Representation on this board is two-thirds from the "public" and one-third from within the higher educational establishment (students and staff included). Each educational unit within the regions is governed by a board with two-thirds representation from within the unit (students and staff) and one-third laymen from outside, appointed by local regional authorities.

Research policy came on the agenda in 1972 when the government formed a commission under the Ministry of Education to investigate the research councils and especially to look into questions of public involvement in the initiation and evaluation of research.[11] In 1975, this commission proposed that the research councils be reorganized to differentiate between research of "societal" and of "scientific" relevance. The commission claimed that lay opinion was indispensable in initiating and evaluating socially relevant research and in making the political choices necessary to balance priorities between scientific and social relevance. Hoping to avoid polarization between researchers and representatives of the public, the commission's recommendations about ways to incorporate lay opinion reflected a compromise labelled as "independence in cooperation."

The new structure, approved by parliament in May 1976, has two administrative levels, the Research Councils themselves and a Research Councils' Coordinating Board responsible for initiating, coordinating, and supporting research in the category labelled "socially relevant." On the board, representatives of public interests have a "dominating influence." Seven of its twelve members, primarily from the parliament, are appointed by government. The other five are appointed by the research councils. These included the councils within the Ministry of Education and from the Agriculture and Forestry Research Council and the Board of Technological Development. The board would have its own budget, estimated at 30 million Swedish crowns in its third fiscal year.

The Research Councils (in the Ministry of Education, this includes councils in the humanities and social sciences, medicine, and natural sciences) are responsible for research mainly of scientific relevance. They remain dominated by academics and researchers. Seven of the ten members are elected representatives from higher educational establishments representing the research community. The other three are appointed by the government to represent research-dependent sectoral organizations. The commission advised, however, that the election of council members from the research community should take place through assemblies that would guarantee the influence of younger researchers as well as established academics, thus broadening representation within the scientific community. The commission also recommended that the councils draw upon outside evaluation groups (from the political parties, labor unions, and industrial organizations) to encourage "evaluation from other than purely scientific aspects."[12] Note that Sweden also has a peer review system in which all judgments are open, but the report proposed increasing the dialogue during the peer review period. As a further link between research and the public, in 1962 the minister appointed a committee of scientists and laymen to discuss long-term research policy. The group meets several times a year, but has, especially in recent years, played a rather minor role, seldom exerting any influence in such decisive matters as the allocation of funds or the setting up of new research organs.

In recommending "wider involvement" in research policy, the commission considered primarily members of parliament plus representatives of administrative authorities responsible for the execution of policy decisions relating to technical affairs. Representatives from the environmental groups that had been openly critical of government science policy were not included. This definition of the "public" reflected the commission's primary objective, which was to find a more effective means to exert political pressure on various government agencies in order to better utilize scientific research and thereby to improve public services. The presence of members of parliament on the Research Board could help to influence the policies of other government authorities whose proposals must eventually go to parliament for approval. Moreover, their presence could also create more favorable parliamentary attitudes toward the funding of scientific research. At the same time, by limiting public representation on the research councils themselves, scientists in universities could be assured a minimum of external intervention.

Parliament passed the commission's proposal to democratize the research councils, but there were some dissenting views. The LO, for example, felt there should be a dominant lay influence in the councils as well as on the board. Some people felt that it was a poor compromise; since the board and the councils had overlapping functions, the dominance of the public in one but not in the other would influence the quality of work supported by each group. Scientists, it was argued, would lean toward any system with the least political interference. Moreover, it was feared that a board staffed with members of parliament could become more responsible to the parliament (with its political and ideological fluctuations and no solid majority) than to the ministries.

Traditionally, the interest in science among parliamentarians has reflected pressures from universities in their districts. More recently, parliamentary interest has tended to expand. In 1974, a parliamentary initiative proposed that the government report annually to parliament on the state of science in every area. Another initiative called for the formation of a parliamentary advisory board on science policy matters. A third emphasized the importance of efforts to bring science information to the public. A commission is evaluating the feasibility of these initiatives, which would further bring political values to bear on science policy decisions.

THE NETHERLANDS

TECHNOLOGY POLICY

As in Sweden, the Dutch government has responded to challenges posed by action groups by attempting to increase public involvement in technological planning and policy decisions. Administrative reforms directed toward democratization had already begun to take place in the Netherlands in several sectors. The Netherlands had created one of the most fully developed systems of workers' councils in Europe.[13] In the field of physical planning, experiments in citizen involvement were under way in the late 1960s. Some were simply devices to tap public opinion, ranging from polls and surveys to the installation of an air pollution telephone complaint system.[14]

The "Progil affair" was an important incident in the development of more direct participatory mechanisms. This dispute called attention to the need to include public opinion at an early stage of decision-making when objectives and intentions of policies were first established. The Progil affair, which began in July 1968, concerned negotiations between the Amsterdam town council and Progil, an industrial firm that wanted to build a carbon-disulfide plant. A group of students protested, circulating a sensational report about the potential environmental and social impact of such a plant. Although a local committee of public officials responsible for environmental health had initially expressed some reservations due to the anticipated stench, it had nonetheless advised going ahead with the construction of this facility. Despite the public concern that followed the students' action, this committee reaffirmed its initial recommendation, stating that adequate measures could prevent calamaties and limit environmental impact. However, in view of increasing conflict, the Amsterdam town council organized three public hearings in March and April 1969. These were well attended by experts, community groups, environmentalists, and political party representatives. Documents and research materials from work groups on both sides of the issue were circulated. During the debate, a newspaper published the findings of an opinion poll: 71 percent of the population opposed the plant and only 9 percent wanted it. The town council then voted against Progil.[15]

This year-long, widely publicized dispute raised many questions about the relative role of national, regional, and municipal governments in deciding the location of large-scale technology-based industries. Following the affair, parliament proposed to the Minister of Physical Planning that new guidelines be established to provide for a participatory process so as to assure a closer interplay between planning requirements and social needs.

The existing (1969) Physical Planning Act had differentiated various levels of planning. At the national level, policy focused on coordination and the establishment of objectives. Provincial states developed plans for the regions after consultation with municipal councils; and the municipal councils adopted "allocation plans" indicating specific intentions for land use in the area. There were also provisions for citizen review; but, as in Sweden, the opportunities for active public involvement were in fact minimal.[16]

In response to the parliamentary proposal, the Min-

ister of Housing and Physical Planning presented a White
Paper (September 1972) to the second chamber of the
parliament, stating:

> The government considers it of great importance that deci-
> sions affecting the physical structure and quality of the
> human environment are not taken until such time as every-
> one whose environment is affected has had an opportunity
> of contributing his share towards the philosophy underlying
> the policy.[17]

The White Paper declared that planning must confront more realistically the problems posed by shortage
of space, facilities, and resources. The need to assess
priorities required political participation by all interests
affected by government policy, for the conflicts between economic and ecological interests, between the
interests of present and future generations, between
individuals and the collectivity, are "not so much technical, but of a political nature."

In his White Paper, the Minister recommended
that, in addition to opportunities for review and appeal,
there must be public involvement during the development of the basic principles and objectives that underlie
the development of specific plans. Thus, national government decisions concerning the physical structure of
the environment, including the construction of nuclear
power plants, must be guided by procedures ensuring
participation.

The White Paper, eventually approved by parliament, set up a system in which all government plans
(and this includes the nuclear power program) are pre-
ceded by the publication of "policy intentions." The
statement of intentions deals with political and philo-

sophical questions: the objectives of economic and industrial growth, the social goals of particular projects, and their likely impacts. These policy intentions are widely distributed for public comment in a process that takes about one year.

The relevant minister in specific planning sectors first consults with the provincial and municipal councils in order to develop a provisional plan stated as a policy intention. This is published and distributed to schools and libraries, and advertised in local papers. Provincial and municipal governments organize discussion groups to interest "the man in the street" and to call attention to his personal interests in the plan. Information evenings (approximately forty evenings for each proposal), photo and sound shows, expert lectures, and television programs present alternatives and explain the ministerial preference. People are invited to send written comments directly to the minister.

All public recommendations and reactions go to an Advisory Physical Planning Council, a representative advisory group that includes "principal categories from society"—that is, workers, employers, and members of voluntary organizations and housing associations. This council conducts public hearings on the issues, summarizes and analyzes the objections expressed, and makes recommendations. The council report is then recirculated to guard against the risk of manipulating the public response in the course of summarizing it. The material then goes to the appropriate ministers, who must respond to criticism, either defending or adjusting the proposed plan. Ultimately, it is the minister who must resolve conflicts between local and national needs by publicly justifying his intentions (in terms of a balanced growth policy.

Ministerial recommendations and all the public documentation goes to the parliament, where a final decision is taken in the second chamber. Citizens can, of course, lobby during this phase of deliberation, but parliament usually follows ministerial recommendations. Three months must pass between the time of the announced decision and its implementation in order to allow for further public comment. Once passed, however, the statement of "policy intention" becomes the basis for the more specific plans at the regional and municipal levels.

The above procedures began with physical planning issues (e.g., decisions concerning which areas should be industrialized, the location of "green spaces," etc.). But they are also used for "structure schemes"—systems for planning in major technological sectors, such as transportation, communication, and energy. Just as in the physical planning process, general policy intentions and tentative plans with their possible consequences are circulated every five years for public feedback. One "structure scheme" has dealt with the development of electrical energy facilities (excluding nuclear power, which will be the topic of a separate structure scheme). Eight public hearings, held in four locations, elicited 150 written comments, some from environmental organizations and federations and some from individuals. The comments concerned a great variety of issues: the future of society and the economy, the need for growth, alternative sources of energy, decentralization versus centralization of sites, and the level of tolerable social impact.

The Dutch government, in implementing this process, expects to reduce the level of conflict concerning specific projects. It is assumed that once decisions are made concerning objectives and people are familiar with general guidelines and intentions, they are likely to accept specific projects that are based upon them. However, some administrators are worried that the situation may be quite otherwise—that public access to information will arouse more concern than previously existed. "Where will it end?" "Parliament already exists as a representative body." "Expanded public participation may only obstruct technological change." More optimistic observers in Holland suggest that one result could be a real increase in public interest in planning at the local level. Viewing this as positive in its own right, they hope to promote public involvement in national issues such as research policy as a means to establish priorities that would relate science to social needs.

SCIENCE POLICY

In 1973, the government of the Netherlands included, for the first time, a ministry with specific responsibility for coordinating scientific research and development. The government established the office of Minister for Science Policy (in the Ministry of Education and Science) at a time when R&D expenditures had levelled off, requiring careful consideration of conflicting priorities. (In 1974, the government spent 2 billion guilder on R&D, 3.6 percent of the total government expenditures. Industry also spent 2 billion.) Demands for limited resources generated questions about the appropriateness of a system in which initiatives for the direction of scientific research, heavily subsidized by the government, came largely from within the scientific community.

A precedent for democratization existed in the educational sector. The University Reorganization Act of 1970 established a system of university governance through a representative council. The act of 1970 also established a governing council with five-sixths elected representatives from academic and nonacademic staff and students and one-sixth representatives from "society at large," appointed by the Crown. The act also set up faculty councils in each discipline, responsible for teaching and research with representatives from faculty, students, and nonacademic staff. This act has raised controversy with respect to how appointments are to be made and what criteria for qualifications should be. It was also criticized by some because it did not meet their demands for direct democracy and by others more concerned with academic freedom. There have been similar efforts to democratize laboratory research by groups of scientific research workers, hoping to broaden the concerns of scientists with social issues.[18]

In December 1974, the newly appointed minister, Mr. F.H.P. Trip, presented a memorandum on science policy to the parliament, proposing a new approach to research policy.[19] This memorandum, a product of consultation with research institutions and professional and industrial organizations, stated as objectives: to direct research toward social priorities, to maintain quality and efficiency, and to democratize the science policy process. Increased public involvement was conceived as a way to develop priorities, to clarify what in fact are the needs of society. The government, according to the memorandum, cannot claim to fully interpret social needs; there must be scope for direct public intervention through the inclusion of consumers or users in the consultative process in which R&D decisions are made. In addition, ministry officials hoped that greater consumer involvement would create more favorable conditions for the implementation of research findings at a later stage. It was also considered necessary to include researchers themselves as participants in the policy process in order to achieve a better balance between scientific autonomy and social demands.

Thus, the memorandum proposed a tripartite system in which research workers, government representatives, and future consumers of research participate in an open planning process, to guide work in applied areas. Councils in ten to fifteen different sectors (energy, health, agriculture, urban planning, development assistance, etc.) include representatives of research institutions actually working in each sector, representatives of responsible government ministries, and representatives of consumers (producer organizations, industries[20], professional organizations, consumer organizations and environmental citizen action groups).[21]

The Minister for Science Policy is particularly concerned that the councils represent the interest of environmental groups as well as industrial consumers, finding an informed and critical scrutiny of government policy to be useful. He has proposed subsidizing environmental groups either by developing scientific bureaus within the government to do research requested by outside groups, or by providing the major groups with their own research capacity. He has also included opposition groups on advisory councils; the National Steering Group for Energy Research, for example, includes two people from the anti-nuclear movement.

The sectoral councils recommended by the science

policy memorandum advise ministers on research policy and outline multiyear plans and intentions (similar to the physical planning schemes). The reports of these councils, including minority views, are to be published for public reaction.

The memorandum deals primarily with nonuniversity research, for there was strong resistance to applying such procedures to decisions concerning basic research. In the case of government-funded basic research in universities, the Council for Scientific Research submits an annual program to the minister. This is available for public review but involves no participation in its development. With this concession to the scientific community, the ministerial memorandum was presented to parliament in December 1974. Parliament invited written reactions and greater specification, and approved the memorandum in June 1976.

If citizens are to be really involved in policy decisions concerning science and technology, they must have an adequate understanding of scientific and technical matters. To this end, in January 1975, the Ministry of Science established a program to translate scientific material on currently important topics for public consumption.

At the University of Amsterdam a course has been organized to teach scientists how to popularize their research findings. In the first recruitment for this course, 31 scientists applied and 12 were accepted (the plan is to train 24 students a year). The students contribute about $37.00; the rest is subsidized. There are plans to start similar courses in other universities.

In Utrecht, a course has been organized for working journalists who wish to broaden their knowledge of science and technology. The government plans to work jointly with publishers, assuming that sharing the cost will stimulate their commitment to publish scientific material.

A television course is being offered through an educational station. This course consists of forty lessons on contemporary science topics (these have included the sea, stress, radiation, aggression in traffic, pollution detection, solar energy, the effect of television on children, astronomy and neurology). The programs provide general information, ranging from pure science to applied science and engineering. The media presentation is supplemented by a subscription program costing $12.00, which includes books and materials coordinated with the programs. For the first series, which began in January 1976, 2,600 people subscribed. A parallel program is presented on the radio with the addition of a system of telephoned questions. All questions are answered in writing; the most interesting ones are discussed on the air. An additional program feature is a series of lectures and discussions in cities throughout the country. Lecturers travel around using video tapes to stimulate discussions.

Finally, to investigate new projects, the ministry has given the Academy of Sciences about $110,000 to develop programs to disseminate information to people in factories and in communities about how science and technology will affect their interests.

AUSTRIA

TECHNOLOGY POLICY

In Austria, as in the Netherlands and Sweden, traditional attitudes toward conflict influenced governmental efforts to increase public involvement in technological decisions. Chancellor Kreisky's response to the nuclear debate by campaigning to open public discussion on the issue is part of a more general policy of organizational reform in Austria. This has been reflected in the internal reorganization of traditional organizations such as industrial firms and the universities, and also in a general commitment to expose conflicting points of view prior to implementing technological or social change.[22]

The Ministry of Industry is responsible for the organization of the energy campaign. Its first problem has been to organize the debate in such a way that opponents and supporters of the nuclear program would have an equal voice. Austrian officials examined the Swedish program of study circles as a possible model, but felt that it had failed to fairly reflect the breadth of opposing points of view or to adequately distinguish the various levels of the technical and political arguments. Thus, in order to provide a basis for a fair debate, the ministry has asked those scientists who have actively expressed their opposition to nuclear power to prepare a list of all questions that must be considered before making a decision on the nuclear program. This list has been divided into ten themes: social and economic questions, cost effectiveness, general problems of energy policy, specific problems unique to Austria, risk evaluation, security, control of nuclear power and its impact on the evolution of society, radiation and waste disposal, cooling, and biomedical questions. Teams of experts, equally divided between supporters and opponents of the nuclear program, are preparing information on each theme. These experts are also considering each question on the original list to explore the degree of scientific consensus. Those issues on which they cannot agree are the topics of discussion in public televised debates taking place throughout Austria. The public presents questions in writing, which will either be answered at the debate or introduced into the proceedings.

One critical issue has concerned the choice of experts to be involved in this information campaign. While it is assumed that most scientists have opinions on the general issue, all participants must be free from specific vested interests. Those who work for industrial firms involved in the nuclear program are automatically excluded.

This, however, creates significant problems, for most scientists knowledgeable in the field of nuclear energy are in fact linked either to research or to industrial applications in the field. Moreover, the problems of security and risk are perceived quite differently by diverse parts of the scientific community: Physicists focusing on possibilities of accidents have different views from biologists, who dwell on the potential long-term hereditary effects of radiation exposure. A number of social scientists view the debates, which focus on safety, as a means to mask long-term economic and political implications of nuclear power. They feel it fosters capital-intensive development which could reduce national economic control and encourage foreign influence.[23]

While grappling with the choice of experts, the ministry is also trying to prepare the public to follow the technical discussion. A dictionary has been written to define all the technical and economic terms used in the discussion at a level which corresponds to the literacy of public school graduates. It is freely available to all Austrian citizens.[24]

Ultimately, the debates will result in a final report on the opinions expressed during public discussions. This will be submitted to parliament by 1978. The report, to be written by participating "experts," is not intended to recommend specific policies, but to clarify which problems in the scientific debate are resolved and which remain open and controversial. In a subsequent vote on the nuclear program, parliamentarians will be freed from the "party contraint" (in the Austrian parliament, each deputy must vote with his party), thus assuming personal responsibility for assessing the risks of a nuclear program.

The Austrian experiment stresses education and the formation of informed public opinion through open discussion. Once informed, however, the population is given no direct power to influence the final parliamentary decision; it can only indirectly influence parliament through elections or through the extent to which the established associations reflect the attitudes of their constituency.

Reactions to the information campaign therefore have been somewhat ambivalent. Some critics have described it as a tactical move on the part of the government to avoid taking a controversial decision before the national elections in October 1976. In fact, the 60,000 signatures collected by the action groups in Sankt Panthaleon corresponded to two seats in parliament. Industrial, business, and administrative interests were optimistic, assuming that increased information would demonstrate that the risks of nuclear power are exaggerated by the action groups and the mass media. They welcomed the campaign as "a breather" after the previous critical attacks on the nuclear program. But at the same time,

they feared that the campaign could increase opposition.[25]

The action groups, on the other hand, pointed out
that the campaign was controlled by the Ministry of
Industry, which is heavily influenced by vested industrial interests. Initially, they admitted that the preparation of the campaign guaranteed a certain balance and
equity in presenting various arguments. They anticipated that the problems that remain unresolved after
the expert debates and changes in public opinion will
force those politicians and organizations still uncom-
mitted to take a stand against nuclear energy. For, prior
to the campaign, not a single powerful political institution or organization had clearly objected to nuclear
energy despite the public concern growing out of the
dispute over Sankt Panthaleon. The only cautious statement came from the Workers' Chamber, asking for more
environmental and security considerations before the
construction of power plants.[26]

Austrian officials feel that their campaign can demonstrate how to reconcile contradictions between expertise and democracy. It will show that experts can be
confronted and forced to state the limits of their expertise, and provide a better basis for political decisions.
Thus, they expected the debates to neutralize the issue.
However, as the public debates began in October 1976,
the first discussions on the more general social and
economic issues suggested that increased information
has tended to increase conflict. In one of the early
debates in Linz, the audience (mostly anti-nuclear) objected to the debate's orientation, and called for a new
chairman to pose other issues for discussion. The media
reported the sharpness of the conflict and the lack of

proposed alternate solutions. By late spring 1977, it was clear that, despite efforts to represent many points of view, the nuclear critics would not accept the context in which debate was limited to those experts selected by the government. They have called for more direct public involvement and proposed initiating the referendum procedure to elicit a direct public response.

SCIENCE POLICY

Discussions of "social relevance" as a criterion for the establishment of research priorities in Austria has also raised the question of broader participation in science policy decisions. Democratization of universities was the first reform to this end, affecting both educational and research functions. The university reform (Universitätsorganizationsgesetz), in 1974 merged some of the institutes and created larger units to stimulate collective and interdisciplinary research, and introduced the participation of scientific personnel (other than professors), students, and nonscientific personnel into decision-making on all levels.

The Ministry of Science and Research, established in 1970, proposed that the university reorganization be complemented by legislation concerning research organizations that would influence priorities in nonacademic research institutions as well. The ministry is preparing legislation which will include a broader representation of "clients and interested groups" in decisions concerning the allocation of public research funds. These changes are intended to gain the public support that would allow redirection of research.

Participatory tactics were also used to implement research policies in the field of health. In 1971, the Chancellor financed a critical analysis of the Austrian health system. The report, published in 1975, criticized the dominant power of the medical profession, the government health bureaucracy, and the pharmaceutical industry, and proposed a reorientation of health research and delivery that would emphasize prevention.[27] The report suggested that this would require participatory processes in all decisions concerning health (including research as well as health delivery) in order to overcome the strongly entrenched vested interests in this social policy area. The proposals, widely publicized, have engaged health officials and researchers in public discussions on television and in the major newspapers.[28] Based on the report, a group of physicians, critical of the current health system, formed an Association of Critical Medicine. This association aims to promote a medicine oriented toward "people's needs" and in opposition to the "corporate policy" of the official chamber of the medical profession. Several adult education associations and the trade unions have sponsored over 150 discussions about the health issues, involving clients, researchers, and medical workers. The intention is to use this kind of pressure to implement necessary changes in both the research and the delivery systems.

NOTES

1. Clearly, many decisions concerning technological development are made incrementally as a result of industrial policy. This process, with

all its political implications for the allocation of resources is, in most cases, outside the sphere of direct governmental control. A major but unresolved problem for those concerned with industrial accountability is how to extend participatory control to this area.

2. International Atomic Energy Agency (1976).

3. National Science Foundation (1976).

4. Levin (1975).

5. The government also had formed, in December 1973, an energy council, a group of about fifty people selected to reflect diverse interests. This council held a series of four public hearings from November 1974 to February 1975, including representatives from activist groups opposed to nuclear power as well as industrial and academic specialists supporting the program. The hearings focused on problems of nuclear power, short-term conservation and supply prospects, and long-term energy policy alternatives.

6. Levin (1975: 10).

7. Levin (1975), reporting an evaluation by the National Board of Civic Information.

8. Study by Gothenburgh University, Department of Political Science.

9. Haggroth (1973, 1976). In 1972, the government made an effort to encourage public involvement with respect to the location of industries. Material presenting options was prepared and newspapers announced its availability and the government's desire for public comment. This experiment was a precedent for later efforts, but no evaluation is available concerning the extent to which citizens responded by ordering the material and commenting on it.

10. Dorfer (1974).

11. Swedish Government Commission on the Organisation of Research Councils (1975).

12. Swedish Government Commission on the Organisation of Research Councils (1975: 34).

13. Business International (1974).

14. In 1967, in Rijnmond, a telephone service was set up to route complaints to a central air pollution control room. The complaints increased as follows:

	1968	1969	1970
First quarter of year	286	787	1 736
Second quarter	308	1 574	3 205
Third quarter	620	2 845	
Fourth quarter	1 218	2 500	

Source: de Kool (1972).

15. Van Rijn (1972).

16. Hammett (1975).

17. Ministry of Housing and Physical Planning, the Netherlands (1972).

18. Daalder (1974); Rip and Boeker (1975).

19. Minister of Science, Memorandum, December 1974.

20. Industry R&D activities are outside the sphere of government control, but it was hoped that their participation in councils would influence their own activities.

21. Discussion paper elaborating the concept of sectoral councils. (Mimeo of early draft, 1976).

22. This is required by the division of authority for regional planning between the federation, the Länder, and the community councils. (OECD, 1975).

23. Blau (1975); Frank (1975).

24. Bundespressedienst, *Kernenergie-ein Problem unserer Was jeder davon wissen soll*, Wien, 1976.

25. During the actions against the plant in Sankt Panthaleon, the company responsible for planning nuclear power plants tried to improve its information policy to counteract the action groups, providing information to local populations, travel for the members of concerned community councils to German and Swiss power plants, and advice in technical matters to the mass media. Only in a few cases were these offers accepted.

26. See: Stellungnahme des "osterreichischen Arbeiterkammertages zum Entwarf eines Energieplanes," 28th November, 1974.

27. Institut für Höhere Studien (1975).

28. The importance of the discussion can be indicated by the newspapers which published parts of the report: the official organ of the governing socialist party *(Arbeiterzeitung)*, an independent newspaper with the highest diffusion *(Kronenzeitung)*, and a newsmagazine *(Profil)*.

The Politics of

WHY THE CONCERN with democratization in the 1970s? And, in particular, why the interest in participation in science and technology policy—the traditional domain of expertise? Resistance to science and technology is certainly not a new phenomenon. Dr. Frankenstein, Dr. Faustus, and Dr. Strangelove are all but reflections of a popular image. The nineteenth-century railroads provoked concerns with the impact of technology on public health, and mechanization provoked the Luddites. The recent erosion of faith in science and technology, however, represents a somewhat different issue, in part because of their scale and impact, in part because of their dominance as central institutions in modern society. Contemporary resistance to technological change is thus often marked by hostility to public bureaucracies and resentment of impersonal, expertise-

Participation

dominated policies. The issue is no longer simply the social or environmental impact of science and technology, but the locus of power and control over major public decisions.

This has been especially evident in the debates over nuclear energy policy. More than any other issue, this has stimulated widespread and fundamental discussion about the objectives of science and technology, the implication of continued economic growth, and the role of the citizen in decisions concerning important technologies. The nuclear debate symbolized a shift from technical to political perspectives; the question of greatest importance to nuclear critics is not the probability of nuclear accidents nor the level of risks, but whether the risks are worth the benefits and whether the continued acceleration of industrial growth "at any speed" is prudent, or, indeed, desirable. Technical competence is no longer accepted as the only basis for deciding such issues, "too important to be left to experts."

In the three countries studied in this report, several conditions converged to provoke a political response in the form of advanced experiments in expanding public involvement in technical decisions. The governments in Sweden, the Netherlands, and Austria are all sensitive to the growing political hostility toward science and technology. In each country, the environmental ethic had been expressed in the formation of action groups increasingly critical of governmental capacity to respond to public concerns. The proliferation of administrative bureaucracies, especially in technical areas, had widened the gap between the citizenry and its political representatives.

In Sweden, just when the environmental movement began to provoke public interest in influencing technological policies, reorganization of municipal government reduced the number of elected representatives and decreased the direct political contacts of the individual. In the Netherlands, the increased importance of centralized physical planning threatened to have the same effect. Attitudes crystallized during particular incidents (the battle of the elms in Sweden, the Progil affair in the Netherlands, and urban reconstruction issues in Austria). The success of protesters in each of these cases stimulated further citizen efforts to influence public policy decisions.

Government sensitivity to protest was reinforced by the balance of power in the parliament. In Sweden, the government was faced with significant criticism from the Center Party with its anti-technology, anti-bureaucracy, and anti-urban ideology. The Dutch Social Democratic Party, in power only since 1973, has held a narrow margin of support which it must maintain through careful accommodation to the pluralistic political demands in that society. In Austria, the nuclear debate occurred just prior to national elections, when the absolute majority of the governing Socialist Party was in question. The 60,000 signatures collected by the forces opposing the nuclear policy would correspond to two seats in parliament, exactly the margin of the Socialist majority, which holds 93 out of 183 seats.

Moreover, in all three governments, there remains considerable concern that further technological development will require greater public confidence, which must be restored through increased involvement in technical policy decisions. The specific response in terms of broadening public involvement was conditioned by the dual goals of economic development and greater democratic participation intrinsic to the Social Democratic image. The leadership has considered the anti-nuclear movement a threat to the industrial growth that it believes necessary to meet its priorities for economic redistribution.

The experiments in participation thus represent an effort to broaden public interest in technological decisions beyond the middle-class action groups in the hopes that government policies would be perceived to be in the economic interest of the working-class majority. At the same time, broader participation was a means to meet potentially disruptive criticism of the centralization of authority and declining influence of the citizen. Thus, the governments of Sweden, the Netherlands, and Austria sought to broaden public participation as a practical means to implement social and technological change, as well as to reinforce their own stability.

Where the experiences of these three countries has differed is mainly in their assumptions about who should participate in expanded programs of public involvement. These differences appear to depend on the ways in which they have traditionally accommodated opposition and conflict.

We have noted that Sweden is a relatively homogeneous society with few basic cleavages and limited organized activity at the local level that would conflict with national interests. It is highly organized through popular movements, and there are well-entrenched channels for their participation. Long-standing government relationships with the major associations has helped to maintain a low level of conflict, for there have been sufficient means by which to negotiate necessary compromise and thus to avoid disruption. In this political context of consensus and compromise, the action groups could only operate outside the normal political machinery, "occupying the elms" and suing the government.

Emulating the environmental movement in the United States but with limited access to judicial courts or public hearings—mechanisms of adversary politics that are characteristic of the American scene—the Swedish action groups set themselves up as an adversary movement questioning the government's decision-making process as well as its policies. With their political as well as environmental goals, they provided considerable pressure on the Swedish system.

The Netherlands, on the other hand, has had a long tradition of conflict and cleavage reflecting religious and regional differences and a history of local political autonomy in its regions and municipalities. Even the most technical issues became the focus of intense political discussion. The nuclear debate was just one more area of conflict, and it did not create the polarization between government and its critics that characterized the Swedish situation. This may be due to the fact that conflict is an old story, and accommodation second nature in a government forced to satisfy pluralist and often conflicting interests.

The political context of public participation in Austria lies somewhere in between the Netherlands and Sweden. Committed by historical experience to avoid conflict, Austria has, like Sweden, a high level of organization and established mechanisms to channel the diverse interests of organized groups. However, the federal structure in Austria and the importance of local autonomy still create a potential for conflict and division. Participatory experiments must therefore try to accommodate diverse demands from different political levels (the Land and the local authorities).

These varying political contexts lead to some often subtle differences in the emphasis of government-initiated participatory programs. Sweden's efforts appeared to emphasize the need to enhance government power in order to better provide public services. By expanding public involvement through the "study circles," the Swedish government attempted to reduce hostility toward technology in order to strengthen its ability to provide energy. Although differences of opinion prevailed among different groups organizing the study circles, they were not perceived as an adversary process. It was fully expected that more favorable public attitudes toward government policies would emerge, given increased public understanding of policy alternatives. Similarly, the program of participation in science policy is intended to create a more favorable attitude within government departments, in industry and in the major organizations, in order to improve research performance. Accordingly, increased political participation mostly took the form of adding members of parliament or the leaders of established groups to government committees. Both education and public consultation experiments were channelled through the existing, large, hierarchical, popular movements which serve to mediate between the population and the political leadership. Thus, Sweden mostly expanded its existing mechanisms for participation through the popular organizations with their well-established elites. The very strength of these existing mechanisms constrained adversary politics.

The Netherlands, however, must accommodate the demands of diverse interests. Here the major emphasis in the participatory experiments has been to find means to develop public consensus about the basic objectives of technological development. This follows from the need to establish reasonable priorities based on the diverse demands of a pluralist society. The most striking characteristic of the Dutch experiments is this effort to incorporate broad public opinion at the earliest stage of policy-making, when objectives are first articulated as "policy intentions." Experiments have also brought activists openly opposed to government policies directly into advisory groups to give the opposition ways to respond within the system. Conflict is expected and accepted as a political reality. The toleration of opposing interests in the Netherlands is further reflected in the willingness of scientists to openly challenge government policies.

Austrian experiments seem to emphasize several goals; public involvement is a way to implement government policies, but also a means to clarify conflicting points of view in order to formulate policy. Accordingly, as in the Netherlands, the Austrian experiments focus on incorporating conflict. It is the opponents of nuclear power who formulated the questions that serve as the basis for the public nuclear discussions. Those with clearly vested interests in the nuclear program are excluded from the debate.

It is too early to evaluate these preliminary efforts to reconcile technical complexity with a broadened democratic participation in science and technology policy. However, the initial discussions in these three countries do provide some insight into the issues involved in implementing a commitment to public participation.

First, *democratization requires participation at an early stage of the policy process.* In all three countries, previous participatory mechanisms were considered inadequate because they were primarily reactive; that is, they allowed only for public reaction to policies already formulated. Experiments emphasize the need for participation in the formation of initial policy intentions and objectives on the assumption that this is necessary if technology is to really reflect social priorities.

Second, regardless of their technical nature, *political conflict and ambiguity are basic realities of technological decisions.* This is evident in the many recent controversies over technological change. Controversies develop over the potential impacts of science and technology and the increasingly centralized and expert-dominated planning associated with technical complexity. While some questions may be purely technical and resolved through better information, most issues raise questions of values and priorities appropriate for political negotiation and thus a broader public involvement. For example, the energy experiments described in the case of Sweden did not significantly change public attitudes; the assumptions about consensus and the reliance on established interests failed to resolve differences, and their persistence eventually led to the change in government. This suggests that the usual decision-making process in this policy arena is unrealistic—an example of how *not* to develop policies for technology. Fully formed plans in this highly sensitive area have been thrust upon the public as if they are purely non-controversial, technical decisions. While even critics often view the technical work on safety as competent, there simply has been insufficient public communication. A more realistic handling of political questions through a more open decision-making process would probably not have avoided conflict, but it might have reduced the mistrust and hostility that has often prevailed in nuclear debates.

Third, if political participation is to be effective, *there must be means to improve public understanding of science.* But efforts to create an informed and interested citizenry confront several problems. People often tend to seek definitive answers from science and are not prepared to accept the uncertainty that is basic to the analysis of the potential impacts of science and technology. There is little evidence that efforts to improve public knowledge about uncertain technical issues have actually reduced conflict. Indeed, evaluations of the Swedish study circles, for example, indicated that more access to information may in fact increase confusion and conflict, for many people are not ready to accept and evaluate the uncertainties inherent in many technical areas. A further problem lies in the difficulty in separating technical information from political attitudes. The fact that many scientists in the Netherlands opposed the nuclear program while few did so in Sweden had little to do with technical questions. Yet, these different attitudes influenced the public debate.

Fourth, *participatory efforts are faced with difficult problems of defining "legitimate" interests.* Who should be involved? Who is representative? Many science and technology questions have no constituency, no immediately threatened neighborhood, no well-defined affected interests. But even when a neighborhood is clearly affected by a technical decision as in the Progil affair, or in the debate over power plant location in Austria, the appropriate locus of decision-making is seldom obvious. Should the siting of an industrial or power plant, for example, be a national, regional, or municipal issue? Differences in the experiments described above suggest that the definition of legitimate interest may depend more on traditional political relationships than on the interests affected by any specific decision.

Finally, *the forms of participation will vary according to the values that a society wishes to maximize.* A major concern in broadening participation is the trade-off between the values of participation and performance. Participation may be cumbersome. Decision-making by fewer participants tends to proceed more quickly. The "structure schemes" initiated in the Netherlands were expected to take about a year before a policy intention could be represented, reformulated, and approved. The information campaign in Austria from its preparation to a parliamentary decision will take three years. The importance of an enlightened public and the clearer articulation of diverse values that emerge from participation must, therefore, be weighed against the necessity of efficiency in the decision-making process.

When there are extraordinary pressures for a rapid decision (e.g., in times of crisis), people accept centralized authority with little attention to democratic values. Speed becomes relatively less important as urgency declines. In practice, this has meant that support for participatory efforts is often a function of age. The young tend to support participation, while many older people, who had developed their careers just after World War II when reconstruction was an overriding concern, worry about delays and obstacles. They argue that long-term perspectives and effective distribution of services require centralization of power within an enlightened administration, accountable to elected representatives. "Are we not going too far?" asked a Dutch administrator. "It is difficult to get anything done in order to make any efficient decision." "Can we really have a Council of the People?" "Parliament is already a representative institution," claimed a Swedish official.

The experiments in participation proceed with a strange mixture of enthusiasm and concern about its implications for the long-term perspectives necessary for technical decision-making. This ambivalence was clearly expressed by an Austrian civil servant: "What is enough democracy? We know from history that an elitist system leads to political catastrophe. Real democracy, wide public participation, can certainly prevent such disasters through the sane instinct of people. But at the same time nobody really knows if it will lead to optimal decisions."

Despite such ambivalence, participatory ideology has been "contagious." Demands for increased public involvement have spread from one sector to another; the experiments in the area of nuclear policy were but a natural extension of administrative reforms directed to democratization in the workplace, in the universities, and in the physical planning sector. These reforms tend to reinforce each other, creating expectations concerning the role of the citizenry. The experiments to date surely represent more an effort to convince the public of the acceptability of government decisions than any real transfer of power. Yet even the limited increase in public discussion has influenced government policies. Indeed, the implementation of public policy and the legitimacy of political authorities may depend on the politics of participation.

References

ANDERSON (Stanley) "Public access to government files in Sweden." *American Journal of Comparative Law* 30, 3, Summer, 1973.

ANTON (Thomas) *Governing Greater Stockholm.* Berkeley: University of California Press, 1975.

ARNSTEIN (Sherry) "The ladder of citizen participation." *Journal of American Institute of Planners*, 1960.

ARZTE "Memorandum betreffend die Errichtung von Kernspaltungskraftwerken." *Osterreichische Arztezeitung*, 25, Oktober, 1970: 2430-2445.

BACHRACH (Peter) *The Theory of Democratic Elitism.* Boston: Little, Brown, 1967.

BLAU (Paul) "Wachstumsperspektiven in Österreich." *Natur und Land* 6, 1975: 175-189.

BUPP (Irvin) and DERIAN (J.C.) "Nuclear reactor safety: The twilight of probability." Manuscript, December, 1975.

BUSINESS INTERNATIONAL *Industrial Democracy in Europe.* Geneva, 1974.

CARROLL (J.) "Participatory technology." *Science*, 19th February, 1971: 647-665.

CASTLES (F.G.) "Political function of groups in Sweden." *Political Studies* 30, 1st March, 1973.

CASTLES (F.G.) "Swedish social democracy." *Political Quarterly* 46, 2, April, 1975.

CAULCOTT (T.H.) and MOUNTFIELD (P.) "Decentralized Administration in Sweden." Public Administration 52, Spring, 1974: 41-53.

DAALDER (H.) and IRWIN (C.) "Interests and institutions in the Netherlands." Annals 413, May, 1974: 58.

DAALDER (H.) "The Dutch universities between new democracy and new management." Minerva 12, 1974: 221-257.

DATA by the Statsvetenskapliga Institutionen, Goteborgs Universitet, March, 1975. (On PUB undersokningen om energipolitiken).

DEN BAK (C.J.) "Democratisation and administrative reorganisation." Planning and Development in the Netherlands 6, 2, 1972: 152.

DE KOOL (A.) "Pollution, policy and people." Planning and Development in the Netherlands 6, 2, 1972.

DORFER (N.H.I.) "Science and technology in Sweden: The Fabians vs Europe." Research Policy 3, 1974: 134-155.

ELVANDER (M.) "Interest groups in Sweden." Annals 413, May, 1974: 27-43.

ERICSSON (Lars Eric) "Reorganisation of local government in Sweden." Mimeo, 1976.

FISCHER (Heinz) Das politische System Österreichs. Wein: Europaverlag, 1974.

FRANK (Wilhelm) "Energiewirtschaft als gesellschaftspolitische dimension." Energie und Wachstum 16, 1975: 23-35.

GARRIS (H. James) "The atomic energy debate in Sweden and the United States." Mimeo draft, 2nd May, 1975. (Annual Conference of the Society for Advancement of Scandinavian Studies).

GELLHORN (Walter) Ombudsmen and Others. Cambridge: Harvard University Press, 1966.

GILLBERG (Bjorn) "Science in the public interest." Symposium on Science in the Contemporary World, Trieste, 17th-20th September, 1974.

HAGGROTH (Sören) "Swedish experiments in citizen participation." Studies of Comparative Local Government 7, 1, Summer, 1973.

HAGGROTH (Sören) "Public participation in design of the environment." Unpublished manuscript, 1976.

HAMMET (Stephen) "Dutch planning." Planner, 6th March, 1975: 102.

HANCOCK (D.M.) Sweden, Politics of Post Industrial Change. Hinsdale, Ill.: Dryden Press, 1972.

HEXSTRA (G.) "Environmental education and public awareness." Planning and Development in the Netherlands, 1973: 140.

INSTITUT FÜR HÖHERE STUDIEN Systemanalyse des österreichischen Gesundheitswesens, 5 volumes, Wien, 1975.

INTERNATIONAL ATOMIC ENERGY AGENCY "A brief report on the

citizen's nuclear energy dialogue in the Federal Republic of Germany." Report 76-1565, 1976.

KORK (Sven) "Supervision in effective hospital wards." Participation and Self-Management 4, 5, Zagreb. (First international conference of self-management, Dubrovnick, 1972).

KOSTELKA (Peter) and UNKART (Ralf) "Vom Stellenwert des Föderalismus in österreich," in Fischer (Heinz) Das politische System österreich. Wien: Europaverlag, 1974: 337-360.

LANGROD (Georges) "Conciliation en Suède du libre accés aux dossiers administratifs." La Revue Administrative 27, 157, January, 1974.

LA PORTE (Todd) and METLAY (Daniel) "They watch and wonder." Report to Ames Research Center, NASA, December, 1975.

LEHMBRUCH (G.) Proporzdemokratie. Politisches System und politische Kultur in der Schweiz und in Osterreich. Tübingen: Springer, 1967.

LEVIN (Tage) "The Swedish 1975 bill on energy policy." Unpublished manuscript, June, 1975. (Report for Statsradsberedningen).

LIJPHART (Arend) The Politics of Accommodation: Pluralism and Democracy in the Netherlands. Berkeley: University of California Press, 1968.

LUNDQUIST (Lennart) "The case of mercury pollution in Sweden." Swedish Natural Science Research Council, 1974a. (Committee on Research Economic Report 4).

LUNDQUIST (Lennart) "Political structures matter in environmental politics." American Behavioral Scientist 17, 5, May-June, 1974b: 731-750.

LUNDQUIST (Lennart) "Sweden's Environment." Planning in Environmental Affairs 2, Winter, 1972: 487-504.

MACHEK (Erich) Die Österreichische Bundesverfassung. Wien: Hippolyt, 1961.

MACRAE (Duncan) "Science and the formation of policy in a democracy." Minerva, April, 1973: 228-242.

MACRAE (Duncan) "Reconciling science and democracy." AAAS Presentation, Chicago, December, 1970.

MATZNER (Egon) "Funktionen der Sozialpartnerschaft," in Fischer (Heinz) Das politische System österreich. Wien: Europaverlag 1974: 429-451.

MAZUR (Alan) "Disputes between experts." Minerva, 11th April, 1975: 243-262.

MERMIN (Samuel) "Participation in governmental processes, in T.R. Pennock and T. Chapman (eds.) Participation in Politics. New York: Lieber Atherton, 1975.

MICHANEK (Ernst) "For and against the welfare state: Swedish experiments." Swedish Institute, Stockholm, 1963. (Under Secretary of Labour).

MINISTRY OF HOUSING AND PHYSICAL PLANNING, The Hague "Some salient points of the Physical Planning Act." October, 1969.

MINISTRY OF HOUSING AND PHYSICAL PLANNING "Publicity observed in preparing the physical planning policy." June, 1973.

MINISTRY OF HOUSING AND PHYSICAL PLANNING "Orientation report on physical planning." February, 1974.

MINISTRY OF HOUSING AND PHYSICAL PLANNING, the Netherlands White Paper, 1972.

MYRDAL (Alva) Towards Equality. Stockholm: Börforlaget, Prisma, 1971.

NASZMACHER (Karl-Heinz) Das österreichische Regierungssystem, Köln-Opladen: Westdeutscher Verlag, 1968.

NATIONAL SCIENCE FOUNDATION Science for the Citizen Program. 1976.

NELKIN (Dorothy) "The political impact of technical expertise." Social Studies of Science 5, 1st January, 1975a: 35-54.

NELKIN (Dorothy) Jetport. New Brunswick, New Jersey: Transaction Books, 1975b.

NELKIN (Dorothy) Nuclear Power and its Critics. Ithaca: Cornell University Press, 1971.

NEUHAUSER (Gertrud) "Die verbandsmäszige Organisation der österreichischen Wirtschaft," in Pütz (Theodor) Verbände und Wirtschaftspolitik in österreich. Berlin, 1966.

NUSZBAUMER (Adolf) Die Stellung des Staates in der Wirtschaft. Wien, 1973.

OBERLEITNER (Wolfgang) Politisches Handbuch Osterreichs, 1945-1972. Wien: österreichischer Bundesverlag, 1972.

OECD Salient Futures in Regional Development Policy in Austria. Paris, 1975.

PASSOW (Shirley) "Stockholm planners discover people power." Journal of American Institute of Planners 39, 1st January, 1973: 23.

PATEMAN (Carol) Participation and Democratic Theory. Cambridge: Cambridge University Press, 1970.

REFLECTION GROUP "A reflection paper on nuclear energy policy in Holland." Anticipation, 20th May, 1975.

RIP (Ari) and BOEKER (E.) "Scientists and social responsibility." Social Studies of Science 5, 1975: 457-484.

SCHIFF (Martin) "Welfare state bureaucracy and democratic control in Sweden." Administration 22, 3, Autumn, 1974.

SCHIFF (Martin) "Sweden today." Current History 68, 403, March, 1975.

SECRETARIAT FOR FUTURE STUDIES *Programme for Future Studies in Sweden.* 1975, p. 16.

SVEDIN (Uno) "Sweden's energy debate." Energy Policy 3, September, 1975: 258.

SWEDISH GOVERNMENT COMMISSION ON THE ORGANISATION OF RESEARCH COUNCILS *Research Councils in Sweden: A Proposal for New Organisation. Stockholm, 1975*

SWEDISH INSTITUTE *Svenska folkets fortroende for Konsumentverket KO oc.* Bjorn GILLBERG, Marknaden, March, 1975.

SWEDISH MINISTRY OF EDUCATION AND CULTURAL AFFAIRS *The Reform of Higher Education,* 1975.

THOMASSEN (J.) "Netherlands Party identification." Acta Politica 10, 1975.

TILTON (Timothy) "Social origins of liberal democracy: The Swedish case." American Political Science Review 68, 2nd June, 1974.

UCAKAR (Karl) "Die Entwicklung des Verbändewesens in Osterreich." Fischer (Heinz) *Das politische System österreich.* Wien: Europaverlag, 1974: 397-420.

VAN PUTTEN (J.) "Konflikten in Nederlandse Politicke." Acta Politica 9, 3rd July, 1974: 257-276.

VAN RIJN (M.) "Progil case." Planning and Development in the Netherlands, 1972.

WEISH (Peter) and GRUBER (Eduard) *Radioaktivität als Krankheitsfaktor.* Wien: Ludwig Boltzmann Institut für Umweltwissenschaften und Naturschutz, 1974.

WEISH (Peter) and GRUBER (Eduard) *Massnahmen zur Lösung des Zielkonflikts zwischen Gersundheitssicherung und Energieplanung.* Wien: Ludwig Boltzmann Institut für Umweltwissenschaften und Naturschutz, 1975.

YBEMA (S.B.) "Redress of grievances in the Netherlands." International Review of Administrative Sciences 39, 1, 1973.

Index

ABOUT THE AUTHOR

DOROTHY NELKIN was born in 1933 in Boston, Massachusetts, USA. She received a B.A. in philosophy from Cornell University in 1954 and worked for many years on the adaptive behavior of marginal groups, focusing on migrant farm workers in the United States. She is associate professor at Cornell University, jointly in the Program on Science, Technology and Society and the Department of City and Regional Planning. Since 1970 she has worked on various social and political dimensions of science and technology. Her books include *Migrant, Nuclear Power and Its Critics, The Politics of Housing Innovation, Methadone Maintenance—A Technological Fix, The University and Military Research, Jetport,* and *Science Textbook Controversies and the Politics of Equal Time.*